CHOICES. CHOICES?
CHOSEN!

by

Anna J. Small Roseboro

Copyright Page

For permissions contact ajroseboro@comcast.net
Cover Art and Section 4 Divider is adapted from a painting
by Manvi Semalty Dehradun, Uttarakhand, India
Interior Photos by Garaud MacTaggart

Scripture quoted may be from the Holy Bible King James Version or may be Scriptures taken from the Holy Bible, New International Reader's Version®, NIV® Copyright © 1995, 1996, 1998, 2014 by Biblica, Inc.™ Used by permission of Zondervan. www.zondervan.com The "NIV" and "New International Reader's Version" are trademarks registered in the United States Patent and Trademark Office by Biblica, Inc.™

Poem "Man with the Holes in His Socks" published in *FINE LINES*: August 2016, Volume 25, Issue 3, p. 214-15

Lyrics for quoted hymns are songs in the public domain. Sources consulted include https://www.pdhymns.com/ and https://hymnary.org. Quotations from George Davis and Shannon "Ingram" Cohen are used by permission.

Music in the video hyperlinked to the electronic version is used with permission of Sonny Brothers Productions, Harlan Sorrell, musicians from Small Church Music, and Hymnary.org.

Please note the in-text citations for other quoted or paraphrased contents. Discussion questions adapted by those posted by Michelle Boudin.

ISBN: 979-8-9911595-0-0

Dedication

To God who prompted the opening scenes and Who
guided the manuscript preparation of the sequels.

To my husband, William, who advised me to consider the historical contexts
of the Scriptures and follow the guidance of the Holy Spirit.

To the contributors who shared verbal and written narratives reflecting
different attitudes and aspects of sexuality
based on the writers understanding of Scripture.

To courageous readers who understand that, as Rudine Sims Bishop told us,
stories may be mirrors, windows or sliding glass doors that allow us to see
ourselves, view others, and even step into a situation for a short time.

To curious readers who recognize the telescope image of
Stephanie Tolliver
who says reading can take us "up close and personal."

Acknowledgments

The multiple perspectives and points of view reflected in this work of Christian fiction could not have occurred without the authentic voices of more than a dozen contributors who wrote for Book One, *TWO, ONE … NOW THREE: How Can That Be?* (2022) and *THREE, TWO, ONE: Time to Run?* (2023)

I thank contributors to Book One and Book Two whose writing flows into this new book. Among the contributors are *Steven Brown, George Davis, Xavier Johnson, Rochelle Jones, Dorien McKay, Alison B. Miller, Kate M. Moore, Michael I. Small Sr., Kayon Tompkins, Mary L. Terry, Gary Ventimiglia, Constance Vickers, and Annette West.*

Three persons who have taken a major role in preparing the manuscript for this book are Michelle Brown, Verneal Y. Mitchell, Rosalyn R. Roseboro, Donna L. Russ, Brooke J. Suiter, and Mary Binion Terry.

I acknowledge and thank the musicians who have shared their music for use in the eBook version of this novel: Sonny Brothers Productions, Harlan Sorrell, musicians from Small Church Music, and Hymnary.org. Clicking the hyperlinks and listening to the music will further enhance the experience of our readers.

And … I acknowledge that none of this writing would be possible without the inspiration of the Holy Spirit and the encouragement of my family to tell the truth. They know the purpose of this series is to write Christian fiction that provides a mirror, window, or sliding glass door through which readers will experience more because they will have seen, heard, and reflected on Lillian's closing question in "The Reveal" in Book One, "What would Jesus do?"

Table of Contents

Copyright Page..2

Dedication..3

Acknowledgments 4

Winter Choices..**8**

    Is This the Time? 9

    How Has This All Come About? 17

    Fun in the Snow? 22

    Are They Ready for This? 27

    Why Is She Calling Me? 34

    Should They Go? 41

    An Anchor or A Buoy? 49

Spring Choices **58**

    What's Upsetting Her? 59

    What's Exciting Her? 70

    Think He'll Do It? 74

    Shall We Worry or Hope? 85

    Can He Walk It Off? 93

    Altar or Alter? 101

    What Purpose or Plan? 109

    You're Gonna Be What? 121

    Is This an Imitation of Life? 129

    Does Poetry Speak for Me? 136

Time for Spring Fling? 143

Summer Choices **148**

Finally, Time to Blossom? 149

Time for Reflection **160**

Reflecting on the Writing and the Message 161

Reflecting on Historical and Theological Ideas 162

About the Author **164**

Winter Choices

Is This the Time?

Louis and Lillian, husband and wife, sit across from one another on this crisp winter evening, each with a laptop straddling their knees. Since Claude left last Summer, this couple has struggled to come to terms with the facts of their life. The two often reflect on what has happened since those startling double Reveals last May: the first, at home when Lillian learns about that relationship, and the second, during a morning worship service, Beth-El Community Church members had learned that Louis and Claude had been intimate partners for nearly two decades.

Outside the Robertson's home, the trees had begun to change colors. No longer light with the fluffy pink blossoms of the crab trees but in the deep burgundies and golds of the autumn. Then came the snow. The leaves that had fallen, blown, and fluttered, looked like valuable jewels caught in the deep green of the pine trees along the side of the house. Those colors did not last long. Now, in January of the new year, the trees are bare, but still standing firm amidst the blowing snow. Sometimes little can be seen or even recalled of the beauty of their lives, the natural, the spiritual, or the personal lives of Lillian and Louis.

Claude, Louis's love partner, chose to leave the country rather than cause the breakup of his lover's marriage and the dissolution of their family. Just as the seasons caused the leaves to fall, the husband and wife now seem to be in a new season in their marriage and wonder if what has fallen is good to be rid of or something they wish was still connected.

The men learned that the truth will set you free, but it also will make you weep. During the Fall, with prayerful counseling, and the support of key church members, Lillian and Louis thought they were on the mend. They even had a church ceremony during which they renewed their marriage vows. But there still are myriad choices they must make to keep the family together.

"Lillian," Louis says softly. "You know that over the years, even though we did not marry for love, but to become legal parents, I've come to appreciate you as a spouse and mother of our children. I'm glad you decided to remain and our marriage to continue. I didn't want a divorce."

Lillian, on the night of the first Reveal, last May, had asked how two could become one, as the Bible said, then become three with Claude added to the circle. Her response shocked him. Louis had been surprised that she cared for him that much to be upset.

"I wasn't sure about that myself.," Lillian answers while wiping the tears from her cheeks with the tissue she's pulled from the box sitting on the table to her right. On that reddish brown table sits the crystal vase Louis had bought for their fifteenth anniversary. Lillian had nearly swept it off the table the night Louis revealed to her his relationship with Claude.

For some reason, since that night, she's left that symbol there. That year, wondering why he had chosen that particular gift, Lillian checked the dictionary. She learned that crystal is the anniversary symbol for fifteen years of marriage. Exploring further, she discovered that a crystal is a three-dimensional network of atoms arranged in a symmetrical pattern. Back then, at the time she received the gift, she saw the three dimensions as standing for their three children. The symmetry, she imagined back then, represented the pattern of their marriage based on Biblical principles.

Little did she know that just two years later she would learn that though solid, crystal could splinter and crack. That seems to be what was happening to them. The admission of her husband's long-term relationship with Claude caused a splinter, a crack in their relationship, but their marriage hasn't split apart. Not yet anyway. Would it remain worth the effort after the children grow up? That's why they had sought counseling. That's why they sit here this evening, doing what they've done all their married life, working together to resolve problems that have to do with their family.

They know they have choices and are free to choose to stay together as a couple for no other reason than to keep the family together so their teenagers can grow up, finish high school, and begin their own lives having been nurtured in a loving home. That, too, has been a problem. The teens love dad's lover, whom they've called Uncle Claude their whole lives.

He had always been around and eventually moved upstairs when just two years ago the family bought their first home, a two-story house on a lovely cul de sac. Last November on Thanksgiving Friday, the family had even streamed the unusual ceremony so Claude could "be there" when Louis and Lillian got married … again. They had even sent to him in South Sedan, Christmas gifts chosen or made especially for him. But, to this day the Robertsons still have times of disarray. Claude Rupert is gone from their house, but not from their hearts.

Tonight, sitting with their laptops, planning to respond to the question Dr. Manguel asked them to write about, Louis and Lillian look across at their spouse. They have chosen not to continue their monthly meetings with this Christian counselor but do continue to journal, using prompts he sends to them by email.

That therapist, who has developed an unexpected admiration for this couple, does not ask them to submit their journal responses because that would mean further payments. But he, too, is concerned about the couple and is confident that if they get bi-weekly reminders in the form of prompts, they are likely to stay on track toward building their marriage on the Rock, Jesus Christ, as they know Him from His Word.

Louis' eyes glide toward the handsome woman he married eighteen years ago but had only revealed to her a year ago that he is bisexual. He had been in a relationship with Claude since before he married Lillian. He'd been loyal to her as his wife, believing that God created him to be attracted to both male and female and as a Christian, he was to devote himself to the woman he married and the children they parented.

That is what he committed to doing and has been faithful to that vow. It was not until Claude had insisted that they tell Lillian about their relationship and asked Louis to move upstairs to live with him that these appalling problems began.

Lillian had trusted her husband to be faithful. He says he has been that. But what does faithful mean to a man who is bisexual? That's what Lillian had hoped time with Dr. Manguel would help her understand. She learned, however, that there is not much reliable research about why men or women are physically attracted to members of their same gender.

One day during the first week after Lillian learned about the intimate relationship between Louis and Claude, her husband had heard on a radio program someone who turned out to be a preacher Louis had known as a teen. It was this minister, Rev. Zusman who suggested the couple seek Christian counseling.

You see, the sermonette had mentioned adultery and that being in a sexual relationship with anyone other than one's wife is adultery. And, adultery is a sin, according to both Old and New Testament Scriptures. Until this time, Louis had not believed he was sinning since he was faithful to each partner.

It had been the marriage counselor and this minister with whom Louis had been communicating who clarified for Lillian and Louis, that as Christians, their main issues were forgiveness and adultery. If they wanted to retain and grow in their relationship with God, have their prayers answered, and be recipients of eternal life in heaven, they had to forgive one another. And if they were to decide to stay married, they must remain monogamous. Period.

"Babe," Louis calls over to Lillian. He had been tapping on his keyboard for nearly fifteen minutes, pouring out his thoughts about the journal prompt. He'd heard Lillian doing the same. She types faster than he because she'd learned keyboarding as part of her preparation for the office job she'd gotten through an internship at college. She now works as an accountant in the same office building as Louis, where they had met as new to town college graduates.

She can touch type without looking at the keyboard. Lillian is fast and she is accurate. Louis is fast and fairly accurate but tends to use just his forefingers and thumbs. His job, as building and security manager, does not require much keyboarding. Mostly listening and giving orders.

Lillian looks up and gives Louis the eye that says, "Give me a moment. I gotta finish this sentence". He goes back to tapping knowing she'd answer when she can give him her attention. Soon, she stops typing, and when he hears no more clicking, he stops, too.

"What?" Lillian responds curiously, leaning back in her leather lounge chair, thankful once again that they'd accepted Claude's advice to get a pair of comfy chairs for the living room. Their house is well-built, but old-fashioned, with no separate family room and no off-limits front room for guests.

"Did you know that Alysa is still getting letters from Claude? I saw the Juba, South Sudan return address on another envelope."

"Yeah, I know." Lillian sighs. "But … you know Lysa misses Claude in a different way than Vyra. He's the one who taught Lysa how to make those weird wooden necklaces."

"Yeah, I know. Alysa and Alvyra spent hours in the shop crafting unique designs that sold well at the GEMS fundraising events. That inter-denominational girls' group has been a lifesaver for Lysa, especially since Vyra is in France for the school year."

The sixteen-year-old twins have always had each other. But Alvyra just could not deal with the family tension and when at the last minute she got accepted to replace the student from their school who was to have gone for the year abroad program, it was difficult for her parents to tell her, "No!"

"Yeah," Louis continues, verbalizing how that plan came together so quickly. "The expenses already had been paid through the patronage of Phyllis' grandfather.

"Thankfully, he didn't renege when Phyllis decided she didn't want to be away from her friends during her junior year. Isn't she one of the GEMS' girls in the drama club?"

"Yeah, she is," Lillian clarifies. "Phyllis wants to be in their final performances because she hopes to become a professional Broadway actress. She says that she never can tell if a scout is in the audience."

"Ha," Louis interjects. "The timing of the whole situation is pretty bizarre."

"I call it an answer to an unprayed prayer," Lillian chuckles. She's recalling one of the devotionals she'd read during her quiet time that reminded her that God knows what we need and if we remain open to His guidance, we will recognize what He provides. Lillian had been worried not just about her marriage but also about the teens. She's a little past worrying, but she certainly still wonders.

Their oldest is a son, Louis Jr., who has been up for a scholarship at their state college. Though not a top athlete, Lou has helped his baseball team win regularly because he is fleet of foot and a good catcher. He is more of a defensive player than a hitter. He usually can make it to first base when he gets a hit, then trusts his teammates to hit enough balls to get him around to home base. Lou also manages to keep his grades up high enough to be an attractive college athlete, too.

The family, however, has begun to notice more raucous behavior from him. He's been stomping downstairs to his basement bedroom and slamming doors. He's the oldest, and is tired of being a model child, student, athlete, and gentleman.

To the surprise of many, including Lillian's older sister, Glendella, Claude has invested money into certificates of deposits at his bank that continue to earn good interest rates. Before he left the country, he had signed them over to Louis and Lillian with the stipulation that the money be held to help fund college expenses for the twins. Claude was confident that Louis and Lillian would be able to handle costs of higher education expenses for at least one of the three children and that should be Louis, their eldest who carries the family names, Louis and Jamal.

He'd not yet decided what he wants to study in college, so his parents recommended that Lou Junior start in the Liberal Arts program, knowing that by the end of his sophomore year, he'd be likely to have completed enough required courses to declare a major to study something specific in his junior year. They don't know the results of the Sokanu/Career Explorer test, which matches student's interests, strengths, and passions with various career paths and job information. The results surprised even him! Why does he believe the family will not accept his decision if he decides not to go to college right after high school?

When Glendella's husband, a life-long military man, met his demise while serving in Afghanistan, it made sense for Glendella to move near her only sister. The widow had had her fill of traveling around the world, wherever her husband had been stationed, and since they'd had no children of their own, she could share the three her sister has. That's what family does … shares. In fact, Claude had signed over to her the lifetime lease he had on the upstairs living quarters, and trusted Glendella's assistance tying up loose ends when he decided to move away so the family would not splinter after the Reveals last May.

Now Glendella wonders when it will be time for her to focus on herself. She's been there for the three teens; she has been there for the two, her baby sister and her husband; she had been there for the one, single man, Claude.

Each member of this extended family is beginning to think: Time to reverse things. One, two, three, they are saying, time for me!

How Has This All Come About?

One Sunday, last May, during altar prayer at Beth-El Community, an inter-denominational church they all attended, Claude had asked the Lord for guidance. Though a little shocked at the answer, he accepted the nudge to go forward. The song that morning had been "Standing in the Need of Prayer." When one of the deacons had come to stand next to Claude and put his arm across his shoulder, this church elder had told Claude, "Just listen".

Claude assumed the deacon meant to listen to the lyrics of the song, so he had. The verse that touched him was

> Not my brother, not my sister,
> but it's me, oh Lord.
> Standing in the need of prayer.

All the time Lillian and Louis had been married, the family had looked on Claude as the play brother of Louis, even though they are racially different. That the family had accepted that relationship is one of the reasons he had been welcomed in their home and fondly called Uncle Claude by the children, now teens.

Lillian had met Claude not long after she had met Louis; they all worked downtown, in the same eight-story business office building and often ate lunch together. Claude and Louis had learned they were alums of the same college, and both were interested in golf. That's how Lillian had known them. Alums and golf buddies.

When the children were born, the three adults, all now, virtually orphans living in a new town, had become family, and Claude was the first call babysitter. He enjoyed the role and became a regular in the Robertson's apartment, attended church with them, and when they moved to their home, moved into the upstairs apartment.

Lillian didn't learn until about a year ago that Claude had helped to fund the down payment on their home and had that lifetime lease on the upstairs flat. These facts made it difficult for the family to understand Claude's decision to leave the country. He would lose so much. But he also had seen how fragile the family became when he and Louis decided to live together upstairs while the rest of the family lived downstairs. He had been blinded by love. Then, moved by love.

His brother and sister-in-law were a couple. The two had become one. He had always been along for the ride, but never the spouse. As Claude had stood at the altar that Sunday last May, he asked the Lord to guide him to do the loving thing. He loved Louis and knew the feeling was mutual. Claude and Louis loved the family and could not understand why they didn't accept the sexuality of their husband and dad and the desire for their brother and uncle just to live upstairs. After all, they'd been lovers for nearly twenty years. Their relationship hadn't hurt anyone.

Their sexual partnership hadn't hurt anyone until that first weekend this past May. Standing at the altar, listening to the song, and then recalibrating his spiritual hearing aid to listen to the Holy Spirit, Claude got the message. He was to do what Christ had done. Sacrifice himself for the people he loved. That did not mean Claude was to give up his physical life, commit suicide, or anything like that.

It was then that Claude realized he was to remove himself from the equation. No more three adults in the family, no more two men who lived intimately. He was to become one. But, just as Claude felt the arm of the deacon on his shoulder, he felt the spirit arm of the Holy Spirit who would be there with Claude wherever the Lord led him. Though he did not receive details at the altar that Sunday, Claude did feel at peace.

He returned down the side aisle of the sanctuary to his seat in the back row next to Louis. The two of them had been ushering that Sunday and all the ushers sat back there during service. Louis was not there. When Claude looked up, he saw Louis walking down the center aisle. He too, had gone forward for prayer that Sunday. And, yes, Lillian, had, too. He then watched her walk up the left side of the sanctuary and climb the stairs back up to the choir stand where she sat until she was to sing later in the service.

That Sunday, her solo with the choir was "Just a Closer Walk with Thee." What a propitious choice for the three of them that first Sunday after Louis came "out of the closet" admitting that relationship to Lillian. Claude was surprised that Lillian could even sing after what she had learned. Then, Claude remembered all of them had been in prayer, and God does answer the sincere prayers of His children. The lyrics stuck with him the remainder of the service and the weeks that followed.

> Thro' this world of toil and snares,
> If I falter, Lord, who cares?
> Who with me my burden shares?
> None but Thee, dear Lord, none but Thee.
>
> Just a closer walk with Thee
> Grant it Jesus is my plea.
> Daily walking close to Thee,
> Let it be, dear Lord, let it be!

******

The teens had been away that first weekend in May, the girls at an overnight with their GEMS group and Lou Jr. at a baseball camp, so all were unaware of what had gone on at home. Claude always came for dinner on the first Sunday of the month and, when the weather was nice, he barbecued on the grill in their spacious, private backyard in the shade of their oak copse.

That Sunday had been no different because Louis and Lillian had chosen to delay for two weeks telling the teens about the change in living arrangements until after the three students had completed those demanding AP exams. Knowing they all hoped to earn high enough grades on these college advanced placement tests to earn college credit, their parents decided to hold off a family meeting to tell the children their dad planned to move upstairs to live with Uncle Claude.

It was during these two weeks that details fell into place for Claude to go to South Sudan. He'd chosen that country for a number of reasons, but mainly because Louis' father had been an immigrant from that country, one of the Sudanese Lost Boys. He'd been fostered by Louis' grandparents who were pastors of a small church across the state from where the Robertsons and Claude lived and worked. Louis' father, Jamal, had impregnated the pastor's teenage daughter, married her, then suddenly died just a few months after Louis was born.

Louis' dad had taken his wife's last name, and so Louis had been named Louis Jamal Robertson and raised by his young, widowed mother who continued living in her parents' home. It was this connection with his Sudanese lover and the fact that the non-profit organization had a connection with the Episcopal church that Claude felt led to check into getting a job there.

Claude had a good work record with an accounting firm and had kept his passport up to date because of frequent trips abroad as part of his job. Then, with the help of Glendella, the widow of an Air Force man, who had connections in New York City, Claude had left town the weekend Lillian and Louis were telling the children about their dad's sexual relationship with Claude.

During that two-week interval between the Reveal to Lillian and then to the children, Claude had met with the Rev. Jackson, the pastor of Beth-El Community, their home church. Claude had come out of the closet with him.

The Pastor had sat in shock, as Claude told him his pain and his plan. Pastor Jackson by that time also had spoken with Lillian and Louis and eagerly supported Claude's decision to demonstrate his faith by leaving town to serve in Christian ministry. He had Claude prepare a video that the Pastor showed at the end of service the last Sunday in May.

In his own words, Claude had announced his reason for leaving the church fellowship and solicited their prayers for him and the Robertsons. Some seated in the sanctuary just nodded their heads that Sunday. They had suspected there was something unusual about that family but never knew what. Others merely sat stunned. The Pastor remained dumbfounded for weeks, wondering how he could explain and apply the Word as members queried him about Biblical teachings regarding sexuality.

Since last Spring, the Robertson, the co-workers, and church family have been challenged to live with the reality that someone they love and respect is a bisexual man, married and the father of three teens. His lover has chosen to leave town, and the family has been experiencing the fallout of that coming out.

What had looked like a model marriage, a Christian family, talented, popular, high achieving teens, active in a nurturing church community has so many in a stir. Can the couple remain together and actually become one family united in Christ? At present the family remains together, but each is wondering if it's time to do what they want to do for themselves. Even after the ups and downs of the past six months, they continue to ask, "What would Jesus do?"

Fun in the Snow?

Today, in the sunny, but cold weather, the Robertson teens are out playing with their neighbor, Andrea Mekonnen's teens who are spending the weekend with her. Her son and daughter attend a boarding school on the East Coast using funds their paternal grandfather provided. His family in Philly had done well and thought that if the young people lived and studied, intermingling daily with people different from themselves, they would more likely be prepared for multiple kinds of good-paying jobs.

Their grandfather was insightful enough to know that young people who managed to remain whole despite the racism they were likely to encounter in even the best school settings, would be ready for whatever they would face later. So, each time a new grandchild was born, this man purchased government certificates of deposit that could only be cashed in when the grandchild reached high school and was admitted to an accredited boarding school. When he died, the cards stopped coming, but his wish now is being fulfilled due to his preplanning.

Though the Robertson and Mekonnen teens have been neighbors for three years, they seldom see much of each other during the school year. When sitting on Andrea's side porch, both sets of teens often ask questions about her and her husband's time in the Peace Corps. That's where they had met and after service got married and started the family. The Robertson teens also like to hear their neighbors' stories of their summer adventures in Martha's Vineyard, not far from Oak's Bluff. One of their enslaved ancestors had been a whaler and somehow his owner legally passed on a plot of land to him, and it has never left the family.

This January weekend, a significant amount of snow has fallen on the yards on the cul-de-sac. The five inches of snow that fell last night provides just what is needed to center the teens' attention on something other than themselves. Each has a secret ornament they will keep stored till the last minute to add to the snowmen and snowwomen they are decorating with pebbles and stones, as well as the typical limbs and leaves from the trees out back. And Dorian the other neighbor on their cul-de-sac has joined them for the frolicking.

Glendella who watches from the window, recalls similar times playing in the snow when her family lived next door to Andrea in their Finger Lakes mobile home community. How surprised Lillian and Andrea had been when during a day working on their soon-to-be first-owned home, Lillian spotted her soon-to-be neighbor watching from her wrap-around side porch. They had not seen each other in decades and spent a little time that day catching up.

Due to other family demands, they've been primarily waving neighbors since. Of course, after the Reveal, Lillian erected walls that let few family members or neighbors inside. She continues to struggle to navigate the cool, stormy times of her marriage. Thankfully, Andrea honors the walls and has not forced her way in even though the three women had been pre-school playmates, then teenage schoolmates in their youth. Oh! Glendella notices the teens are now standing in a row.

******

"Betchu can't guess who this is?" Alysa calls out, standing straight with her hand pointing to the snowperson she's just adorned with a cocky burgundy cap she'd found in a basement closet. By this time the other four have nearly finished their creations and turn to see what the competition will be for their rolled, stacked, and patted snow characters.

"Ah, that ain't nobody!" Dorian exclaims. "What kinna hat is that for this time of year? And in that blah purply blue. You know the high school cross-town school colors is purple and gold."

"Yeah," Alysa replies. "So what! My man got nothing to do with the wanna-beez over there. Com'on. Who you think this is?"

The teens had challenged each other to create someone out of snow that the others would recognize. They worked in a big circle using snow from the lawns of all the neighbors who let them access the white stuff from their yards. For the most part, the teens had been working with their backs to each other and hadn't been paying attention to the assemblages of their competitors. All, however, were pretty sure that Alyssa would win for details. She, after all, is the artist among them.

The teens turn back to their snow statues for a few more moments tapping, patting, and checking stability. Then one by one, they stand behind their snowman or woman and look more carefully at the others in the circle. Not surprisingly, each has some of the same basic features: rocks for eyes, pebbles for lips and buttons, and tree limbs or twigs for arms.

Belinda, Andrea's 18-year-old daughter has wrapped around the head of her snowwoman, a scarf in the form of a sedate African style Gele, but it does have a rather puffy Nigerian style bubble on the side. How strange to see this Kente cloth on a white character. Oh well. Snow is white. Other than the hat, the woman looks rather blasé.

Each of the guys has attempted to create slender snowmen to appear more athletic. This has required them to pound their snowballs and stack them firmly to maintain balance with the fluffy snow they're working with today. No one is surprised that Dorian tried to add color to his statue by patting on brown sand from his mother's side flower garden. Dorian's character has a basketball at his feet and a high school sweatshirt tied around its neck and hanging down the back.

Lou Jr., too, has attempted to create an athletic figure, but his has a pot belly and a whistle hanging around his neck. So, he must be a referee who does not have to run much. They laugh as they envision some of the line judges and referees that they've seen on the televised sports shows.

But it is Horace, Andrea's fourteen-year-old son who has surprised them all. He's the youngest and has been so quiet, that none of the older teens have paid him much attention. His snowman is standing on his head! It is balanced by two branches for arms that give him balance. Horace, a high school freshman, has utilized his understanding of the African builders of the pyramids. He has triangulated the ground touching parts of his snowman: the two arms and head, so his snow person is standing sturdily, his pebble eyes winking up at the other teens.

Lou Jr. pulls out his cell phone and takes photos of each of the builders and their creations. He plans to share them on his social media page and send them to Gramma Ruby and her husband in California. They both used to live in a snow town and will understand the ingenuity of these creations. Mom and Dad will get a kick out of seeing them, too.

The teens never actually name their creations but notice how each of them reflects something about the creator. Whether or not they verbalize, each is genuinely thankful that God, their Creator has sent the snow with which they, as teens, can still have fun.

Lou knows Alyssa's going to want to send copies to Uncle Claude, as well, so before he puts his phone away, he texts the photos to both Alvyra, his other sister now studying in France, and to Uncle Claude over there in South Sudan. Both will be glad the neighbors are having fun but will also miss being there to enjoy the frivolity. Oh well! It was their choice to leave. Soon, it will be Lou Jr.'s turn to do the same. But will he?

Glendella notices Lillian drive up, then stop to open the garage door with the automatic function Louis had installed the first year the two lived here. She, then eases the car into the space reserved for her green Honda. She's been driving it for years and seems reluctant to update or upgrade her mode of transportation.

When teased about driving such an old car, she replies, "It gets me safely to and fro. And, anyway, we're saving for the kids to go to college." Few could argue with that rationale, so Lillian keeps driving her ten-year-old car.

Glendella sighs. The sisters have been drifting apart since Lillian and Louis had the church ceremony to renew their vows or as they say, to restart their marriage. Dr. Manguel, their marriage counselor, had advised them not to attempt to rebuild their marriage as a mosaic with splintering stones and pebbles from the past but to start over, building their marriage on the Rock, Jesus Christ. The couple is finding this easier said than done. Each now wonders if it's time to focus on their own personal needs. Glendella wonders how that will be. She's thinking the same. It's time for me!

Are They Ready for This?

Alvyra has just gotten off the phone talking with Lawrence from Beth-El Community Church. She is smiling a bit at the jokes they shared, and also feeling a little sad that she won't be home for spring break when he'll be in town. He's the son of their Minister of Music and had been manning the sound booth for the service when Alvyra's parents got married … again. She'd flown home from France to be a part of this unusual family event when her parents committed themselves to a lifetime of monogamous faithfulness.

Earlier, at the beginning of the school year, in August, Alvyra had jumped at the chance to leave home when she learned her father and their play Uncle had been lovers all her life. But, while she's been away, her parents had sought professional marriage counseling, and with prayers of family and friends, have forgiven each other … he for not telling her and she for abhorring him because he hadn't.

Now Alvyra is wondering whether or not she, too, can forgive the three of them and get on with her life and stop looking back at what had happened and what, thank the Lord, did not happen. She's not the daughter of divorcees.

While at that marriage ceremony, she and her twin, Alysa had stood up with their dad, in place of a best man. Uncle Claude had filled that role over eighteen years ago. But that's another story. Her brother, Lou Jr. had escorted their mother down the aisle and Aunt Glendella had served as matron of honor. Their only living grandmother, Ruby Robertson and her husband had even flown in from California for the ceremony.

It was Gramma Ruby's first trip back to her home state since the year, when her only son was a college freshman had told her that he is gay. She had no idea he was bisexual and was shocked when she learned about his relationship with Claude.

Back then, being the widowed mother of a homosexual man was more than she could stand, so she'd fled, married a man who'd been asking her to do so for years, and the two of them moved to California to attend seminary. But, at last, she, too, reconciled with her son through the prayers and conversations with Lillian, who reminded her mother-in-law that Agape love is all she needs.

Practicing same-gender intimate relationships is a behavior that Ruby Robertson believes is wrong. But this minister has come to terms with the fact that she need not separate herself forever from her family because they have different beliefs, or understandings of the Bible. She can leave all that to God. For now, she has been struggling to enjoy being the grandmother her only son, Louis, had promised to make her when she admitted to him that having grandchildren was one of her fondest wishes.

Yes, the grands have visited her a couple of times, thanks to her husband who had paid their way. But ... she'd been uncomfortable. Ruby had no respect for the mother of her grandchildren. She thought Lillian had known about Louis' sexual orientation and had married him anyway. But, just a few months ago, she had learned the truth: Lillian had been even more in the dark! She neither knew her husband is gay, nor about the relationship between Louis and Claude. That news seemed even worse than what Ruby had thought all along.

But ... thanks be to God, her husband encouraged her to put into practice what she preached. She had to forgive. He insisted they attend the ceremony which proved a service of reconciliation. The wedding had reunited the family at last. Gramma Ruby had even led the prayer of blessing for the couple and found that she meant it. Her spoken words had come from her heart. The family seemed to enjoy being together with their guards down.

******

Now, Alvyra is back in France, completing her commitment to a program from her high school. This one paid travel, room, and board for students to spend a year abroad honing their skills in reading, writing, and speaking a World language in an area where that is the dominant home and heart language of the citizens there. Alvyra had jumped at the chance to get out of the household in tumult as they sought to understand their dad, Louis, and his choice to marry and father children with Lillian, his wife, and remain in an intimate relationship with his male lover.

This sixteen-year-old had gotten so uptight that she could not stand being in the same room with her parents. Alvyra had wanted to hate them both for making her feel so bad. But she found she couldn't do that. She also couldn't control the tensing of her stomach every time she imagined any kind of sexual intimacy. Now, this teen finds herself attracted to Lawrence and is glad he decided to stay in touch with her after the wedding ceremony last November.

Alvyra had felt an attraction to Lawrence during the rehearsal, the Wednesday before Thanksgiving. The feeling remained, and she winked at him from her place next to her dad that Friday when her parents were kneeling for prayer after exchanging their vows of commitment to one another.

Lawrence had been up in the sound booth streaming the service so that Claude could be a part of this family event. What an odd thing to do! But as Christians, her parents had decided to accept Claude's promise to remain celibate out of love for Louis, and away from the country, out of his love for the family. He had no living relatives and had been a part of the Robertson family since he'd moved to town and met Louis, whom he learned was an alum of the college he'd attended. They both enjoyed playing golf and had begun to spend time together, initially because of these three connections: working in the same downtown office building, being golfers, and alums.

Early in their friendship, Louis learned that Claude is a Christian and a gay man. Claude began attending worship services with Louis and over time, the two men became physically intimate. It was during the second year of their relationship that the two realized they'd never have a family as a male couple. Men were not permitted to marry or to adopt in their state.

Lillian had been friends with Louis and welcomed Claude into their circle of workmates and members of the same congregation. She had had absolutely no idea of the sexuality of either man. They treated her with respect and because of her age, she welcomed the companionship when they accompanied her to social events at the job and at their church. She had no reason to challenge Claude being best man at that first wedding. For the second wedding, he was there as a family member, watching virtually from his new home in Juba, South Sudan.

Alvyra, sitting this Valentine's Day evening, in her bedroom of the French hostess in Loire, France, lets her mind glide to that wedding reception back home at Beth-El church.

******

"Ah," Lawrence says to Alvyra as he gulps the punch from the tiny glass cups the Beth-El hospitality team chose for this reception. They'd decided to use only what was on hand rather than buy paper or plastic cups and plates for this unusual celebration. It was no problem putting these old-fashioned crystal cups all in the two large-capacity dishwashers in the church kitchen. Each has three racks to accommodate lots of small items.

"Hmm," replies Alvyra as she takes a bite from one of the luscious cookies that she'd snagged from the top of the two-tier serving tray set up across the center of a long table next to the wall. The large crystal bowls with the orange-colored punch sit on each end of the tables, where members of the hospitality team take turns pouring the cups ¾ full for celebrants who line up for the tasty refreshments.

"Well, that was really something!" Alvyra continues. "My parents were hoping more folks would show up for their ceremony. But, in the back room where we waited with our dad, we peeked out the door and saw only the front four or five rows were filled and just said, the key folks are here. The bride, groom, their attendants, the Pastor and the musician."

"Yeah, the sanctuary really looked empty from where I was sitting up there in the booth. We didn't have anyone in the choir stand, so it really felt like something was missing. Pops didn't say a word to me about what they had planned as a surprise for your parents. I thought it was rather cruel, but who am I to say? I'm just a college sophomore. You know what they say about sophomores," he quips before taking a bite of his third cookie.

"No, what do they, whoever they are, say?"

"Well, the etymology of sophomore is a pair of Greek words, 'sophos' meaning wise and 'moros' meaning foolish. Sophomores sometimes are teased for foolishly thinking they are smarter than they are!"

"Yeah. I heard that last year in high school. Do they still tease you when you get to college?" She stomps her foot, and snarls, "That's awful!"

"Aw, it's not so bad. If it's not true. And … it's not true about me. I'm wise enough to know that I'm not all that smart. Yet. Alvyra, this first semester is a killer. I got so much homework over the holiday weekend that I almost told my dad I couldn't do the sound today. But the regular tech guy is out of town for the holidays and Dad said the service wouldn't be long. And, he said, it would be a nice break from studying, and I'd get to hear him sing."

"Like you don't know what your dad sounds like singing," Alvyra chuckles. "That's a laugh," then reaches up to catch the crumbs falling from her too-full mouth.

"Well," she continues, "you can imagine how our hearts swelled when we saw those lines of fifty or so folks march in from the side rear doors singing 'Once Again We Come to the House of God'. By the time all dad's usher, baseball team, and men's group pals and their families were seated on the groom's side, and another fifty from mom's women's ministry and choir friends and their families sat on the bride's side, the church was nearly as full as a Sunday morning service."

Lawrence nods his head, strolls back for a refill of his punch cup, and returns to stand next to Alvyra, near one of the entry doors to a Sunday school room. Both had grown up in the congregation and had even been in a couple of multi-grade classes together. He's three years her senior and until this weekend, each had gone their own way, having attended different high schools.

She swallowed, took another drink of punch, and resumed the conversation, reflecting on what they had just witnessed upstairs. "That was quite a song to have for a wedding ceremony." She begins to sing softly, the first verse of the song, and Lawrence hums in harmony.

The love of God is greater far
Than tongue or pen can ever tell.
It goes beyond the highest star
And reaches to the lowest hell.
The guilty pair, bowed down with care
God gave His Son to win.
His erring child He reconciled
And pardoned from his sin.

By the time they get to the chorus, they are singing louder than they imagined.

O love of God, how rich and pure!
How measureless and strong!
It shall forevermore endure
The saints' and angels' song.

The two glance up, their eyes meet, and both blush. It is more obvious on Lawrence because of his white skin, but Alvyra's creamy cheeks turn a peachy color. The two young people look around and see folks nearby giving them the eye and grinning as though they are observing something surprising, but they approve.

Both Alvyra and Lawrence are amused thinking folks are smiling to hear how well they harmonized. Then it hits them. Observers think they are a couple! Both turn away, walk over to the table where they are to place their dirty cups, and end up in the corner together.

Since that encounter, the two have remained in touch virtually, but due to the difference in the time zones in which they live, and the fact that both are conscientious students, they pretty much save phone calls for Sundays… afternoons for Lawrence and early evenings for Alvyra. Because her family regularly calls her on the first and third Sundays, she and Lawrence have gotten in the rhythm and reserve time on the second and fourth Sundays for regular phone conversations. Between times, they text.

Why Is She Calling Me?

While sitting in Sunday School, Glendella gets a phone call. The volume is set to "no ring." so she only sees the message pop up because she is using her cell phone to follow the Scripture for today's lesson. Oh, good grief, she responds silently. It's Mother Grisham. I talked to her yesterday, and she said she didn't need a ride after all. Then, up pops a message from her daughter saying, "Will you please pick up my mom? I gotta work today."

Glendella is frustrated. She's torn between staying for an intriguing Sunday School lesson and putting into practice what they are taught at Beth-El Community Church. Be ready to help when you can. "Ah, shoot. Okay, Lord. I'll go get her," Glendella says quietly as she turns off her phone and slips it into her pocket. She tips out and heads to the parking lot, glad the snow has melted, and the streets are salted and clear.

Mother Grisham has aged rapidly, going from being one of the more physically active senior citizens to being barely mobile. She had slipped on the ice following the Christmas service and has not bounced back as she hoped she would. So, her daughter has been driving her to church each Sunday.

The Beth-El women's group has consented to gather at Mother Grisham's for their regular meetings so she can continue participating without having to get up and get out. This gracious hostess loves company anyway and with members alternating bringing refreshments, she only has to provide cups, plates, and silverware which can all go in the dishwasher afterward.

But today, all Mother Grisham's goodness is doing little to calm Glendella. She was planning to chat with that handsome usher during the fellowship hour. He's about her age and, like her, has no living spouse. Beth-El's membership has grown, and they now offer Sunday School for adults before morning worship and Sunday School for kids, teens, and adults afterward. Glendella has chosen the early time and often stays after service to assist with clearing up after the fellowship gathering between service and late Sunday School.

Today, when she gets to the senior member's house, Mother Grisham is standing in the garage next to her bulky ancient sedan. What's going on? thinks Glendella. That old lady can't move that leg fast enough to drive. But, raised to honor her seniors, Glendella parks her car near the curb in front of the house, prays for patience, and walks up to the garage.

"Oh, thank you, Sweetheart!" Mother Grisham gushes. "So glad you could come get me. I want you to drive my car since I can't climb up into that SUV of yours. My car sits low, so all I have to do is back in and plop down. My visiting nurse showed me how to put a towel on the smooth leather seat so I can swing around easily. The towel does the moving and I just sit on top."

"Sure, Mother Grisham. Let me hold that bag for you so you won't drop anything as you get into the car. Where are the keys?"

"Here you are!" the older lady, just in her late-sixties, hands her driver a straggling bangle of keys on a clunky key ring that includes house keys and the key fob for this majestic old tan car that has clutter all over the back seat. Looks like it hasn't been cleared out since the owner had been doing her mission work, ready with stuff to share whenever she saw a need. There are canned goods and pairs of new mittens lying loose on the floor back there.

Again, remembering that she is to be gracious, Glendella stands quietly as Mother Grisham sits and swings around into the passenger's seat. She tugs up the woolen pants leg to help lift her stiffened leg. She obviously has been practicing because it does not take her long to get settled. She reaches out for her tote bag and nods for Glendella to close the door.

Glendella walks around the rear of the car and up to the driver's side door, takes a deep breath, and slides in to do her Christian duty. She hopes they will arrive on time. Thankfully, this is not her Sunday to be playing the organ for the choir. She and her sister, Lillian, often provide special music on Sundays the gospel chorus leads praise and worship in song. Glendella's mind slips back for just a moment.

******

She recalls that it was on one of those Sundays in May. The dual Reveals about Claude and Louis nearly dismantled the Robertson household. But so often God made His calming presence known in songs, Bible readings, and prayer. He provided a Biblical way out for Claude, who announced that He had decided to follow Jesus. With the power of the Holy Spirit, Claude chose to let love guide his decisions. He sacrificially left the man and family he loved so they could live a life based on the Word that says it is adulterous to be in an intimate physical relationship with anyone other than one's spouse.

Claude seems to have settled nicely on the other side of the world. Unfortunately, it is taking longer for the rest of the family. But, it has been songs like the solo Lillian sang that May Sunday that have helped. That morning after the night before, when she learned about her husband's sexuality, she had sung,

> Just a closer walk with Thee,
> Grant it Jesus is my plea
> Daily walking close to Thee.
> Let it be, dear Lord. Let it be.

******

"Um, Glennie, my dear." Mother Grisham's voice snaps Glendella back to the present. "Will you push in this end of the seat belt? I'm just not as flexible as I used to be," Mother Grisham asks holding up the silvery link end of the seat belt. Glendella pushes aside her bulky winter coat so she can slide the belt into place and then snaps hers in, too. They both are anchored into place.

"Which of these buttons is for your garage door closer?" Glendella asks as she sits with her foot on the brake now that she has backed the car to the street, but not out of the driveway.

"Oh, you remember. It's the little creamy button up there on the left." Mother Grisham seems to have forgotten that this is the first time Glendella has driven this car. She, however, being a widow who had traveled all over the world with her military husband has lots of experience driving different cars, so she's not nervous. She just knows to ask, first.

The two get to church on time, and a different usher than Glendella wanted to see happens to be among the brothers who assist Mother Grisham into the wheelchair the church keeps on hand for times like this. These two folks nod and continue with the series of tasks. Get Mother Grisham's coat off and hang it on the coat rack. Get her settled into the wheelchair, her tote bag hanging from a handle by her side and rolled up to the space set aside for those who attend services in their own or borrowed wheelchairs.

Mother Grisham is no longer embarrassed about arriving this way and smiles at those who turn and nod as she is wheeled past them.

Glendella looks around. Where is he? Isn't this the week for that Cablinasian to usher? She's seen the Tiger Woods' looking guy nearly every week since she moved to town a couple of years ago to be near her sister. While James Milton did not claim to be a mix of Caucasian, black, American Indian, and Asian, he does look enough like this championship golfer, that most initial conversations had him explain his heritage. He and Glendella had that conversation at one of their first Sunday afternoon lunches.

Once her husband, Quentin's bodily remains had been ceremonially buried in Arlington Cemetery after his death in Afghanistan, Glendella had been at a loss. The two of them had accepted Air Force assignments as part of Quentin's promise to see that she got to travel widely.

The two of them had graduated the same year from one of the Finger Lakes community colleges. Both saw little future for them in their hometown, so when Quentin joined the Air Force, he asked Glendella to marry him. He'd committed to remaining a Christian while he fulfilled his family commitment of serving in the military of the country that had welcomed their Panamanian ancestors after their work on the Panama Canal.

Quentin Gonzalez admitted that he needed a wife with him but wasn't particularly interested in being a father! It just so happened, that he had overheard gossip during his college job as a waiter, that she was infertile, and wanted to travel and extend her musical training as a keyboard player of piano or organ. She accepted his proposal. Being parents would not get in the way of either of their dreams. But, alas, he's now dead and buried, but she's alive and well. What now?

Glendella's been moody recently. The last time she looked at herself closely in the mirror, she noticed signs of aging. True, she's not yet fifty years old, but with the death of her husband, her decision to move here to town where her sister lives, then, having to move out of her apartment due to gentrification, and now living upstairs from her sister going through marriage trauma, Glendella has not celebrated a birthday in years. But it's not her birthday itself that's on her mind; it's what happens after that seminal day.

Last November, a couple of weeks before Lillian and Louis had that odd marriage ceremony, Glendella had bumped into an usher and found her heart beating at a speed she imagined only occurred with teens!

Even though she'd married Quentin Gonzalez by choice, it had been a marriage of convenience for them both. They got along well for the twenty-five years before she lost him to a mysterious death, and Glendella never regretted that marriage. And since they knew she was infertile before their marriage, she never worried about being a mother. It is too late for that now anyway, but is there time for a marriage of love?

The man she is interested in, James Milton, is a long-time widower, having lost his wife following injuries in a car crash nearly fifteen years ago. They'd had a couple of children, but his parents had raised them while James returned to college, earned an advanced degree, and worked to provide financial support for the five of them.

He, however, moved here three years ago to accept a better-paying job now that his oldest son is a freshman in college. As are the majority of those attending Beth-El, he is glad to have found a welcoming congregation comprised of men and women like himself, new-to-town, and Christians interested in practicing more congenial faith according to the Word.

In fact, James Milton had been hired by his company to help them develop and nurture more diversity, inclusion, and equity opportunities for the various nationalities of students at the university, where he also is an adjunct professor. Both want James to assist with programming to entice graduates to stay and work for local industries.

The men at Beth-El had urged James to get involved with a ministry right away that would help fill in after-work time in safe ways that would not tempt him to stray from the faith. He'd joined the baseball team and usher board. Neither require much talking, just showing up and doing your job.

James Milton had seen Glendella at the organ on the Sundays she accompanied the gospel chorus, and at some of the social events. But he had not been overly aware of her in any other way until she'd stumbled and bumped into him at that unusual wedding of her sister to her own long-time husband.

Something clicked with Glendella and James. He started asking questions. When he learned she was widowed, too, he knew that Biblically, they both could remarry if they chose to do so. He learned she had no children, so stepbrothers and sisters need not be an issue if he and Glendella decide to pursue a relationship that leads to marriage. But they needed time to get to know one another. Should that be their goal this Spring?

Should They Go?

Lillian left the office that day, all excited and wondered if this would be the time to ask Louis about the idea. During lunch with Lillian, Virginia glowed as the two of them shared a giant turkey sandwich and their own cups of soup.

******

"Guess what my honey gave me for Valentine's Day?"

"I have no idea," Lillian responds as she nibbles a strip of turkey from the sandwich, hoping the lettuce will not slide out, too. She's already eaten her cup of tomato soup purchased from the café but is not satiated because the soup was seasoned rather blandly this week. As she crunches the sesame seed bun, she looks up at Virginia, smiling at her excitement.

"He's gonna take us on a marriage retreat in April. Would you and Louis like to come? It may be just the getaway to help you celebrate the progress you're making and plan for the days ahead."

"I don't know, Virginia. What do you do at a marriage retreat? Louie and I still are in early stages of real reconciliation. We've forgiven each other but are still trying to trust each other. I can feel it sometimes when I get suspicious about things he chooses to do by himself. I always wonder if he's still lonely for Claude."

"He may be, Lillian, but I was at your wedding ceremony when you renewed your vows. I could feel something special that day and from what I've seen around the building, he's on the ball."

"Yeah. You're probably right. Tell me, Virginia, have you and your husband gone on these retreats before? Who comes and where are they usually held?"

"Well, since you ask," Virginia says, glad she has a willing listener, proceeds to lay out the generalities. The one she goes to is offered by Christians, and open as a non-denominational experience for those who have made that commitment to Christ and those who still are open to considering it.

The one she and her husband went to generally is held at one of the mid-range price resorts, before high season prices go into effect. Most places are chosen with the likelihood of nice weather so couples will feel comfortable exploring one of the walking trails, playing tennis or golfing during the free time built into the weekend schedule. Then she pulls a three-fold brochure out of the purse she'd laid in the extra chair at their table along the wall.

"See!" Virginia invites as she opens the brochure. The word Agape draws Lillian's attention right away. Pastor Jackson was always talking about the love of God that is different from sexual love and familial love. Rev. Jackson urges them to let the love of God, agape love, infuse their behavior and flavor their relationships.

Lillian flips to the next page and sees the schedule that includes whole group gatherings at mealtimes, small group topical sessions on Saturday, and gender-specific sharing sessions on Sunday morning, before closing worship services. This Agape Marriage Ministry even offers counseling sessions for couples who request them. Hmmm. Typical of a person who works in the accounting office and who'd been raised to consider financial commitments, Lillian follows her finger sliding down the page till she gets to the price of the weekend.

It is an all-inclusive price that covers two nights, three days, four meals, and access to facilities at the resort. Hmm. Not bad. If they start saving and skimming now, she and Louis could probably afford such a weekend. She'd not get a new Easter outfit this year. That would save a bit, too.

"Who usually comes to such events?" Lillian probes. "Couples in troubled marriages?"

"Well, I'd say many who come the first time may have felt pressures in their relationship, but among the ninety some couples who came last year, most were returnees. Some started coming within their first years, others, later, but many have been coming for twenty years or more. My husband and I will be on our fifth time. We missed a few years when the kids were young, but, hey, now that they're older their parents really need this time away, together!"

"Why do folks keep going to a marriage retreat if their marriage is in good shape?"

"Good question! I'd say because the workshops provide opportunities to consider a variety of challenges to living as Christians in a relationship. The planners know that different issues come up over the years based on where the spouses are in their Christian walk as well as in relationships with family members and at work.

"You see there," Virginia points out, flipping to the page with the schedule, "We have small group workshops on topics that help couples with communicating about financial management, sexual intimacy, blended families, parenting, spiritual growth, as well as biblical roles in marriage. You know from your nearly twenty years with Louis that these issues arise from time to time and in no particular order."

"Wow! What's missing? I can see why couples keep going! The price isn't bad and since one never knows from year to year which sessions will be just right, planning to go regularly probably is worth the investment of money and time."

"You got that right, Lillian. And having time away at a resort with others who have or are dealing with some of these issues helps me and my husband see that we're not all that different. But thanks to the gathering, we always return with ways to help work through whatever it is we're struggling with that year. And you know what is really cool? We sing, sing, sing, sing, sing! Some of us White folks even have our hands raised high in the air!" she chuckles. The two of them often kid each other about stereotypes with which they each live.

"Every general meeting begins with lively songs sometimes chosen to go with the theme for the year. Hey! You like to sing and Louis likes being with you when you do! Hey, do you know this one?" Virginia looks around and sees that others in the dining room are intent on their own conversations or are reading their cell phone messages.

She begins to hum softly, and Lillian begins to sing, equally softly, the two with their heads tilted across the table so they can hear each other without disturbing others:

> Time is filled with swift transition
> Naught on earth unmoved can stand.
> Build your hope on things eternal.
> Hold to God's unchanging hand!

By the time they get to the chorus, the guy at the next table has begun to sing along.

> Hold to His hand, God's unchanging hand.
> Hold to His hand, God's unchanging hand!
> Build your hopes on things eternal,
> Hold to God's unchanging hand!

"Hey, what you two talking 'bout over there? This ain't no church. But I know that song. My Grammama used to sing it all the time." The chunky man has slid his chair nearer to their table.

"Oh, Ralph, I was just telling Lillian about the Valentine's gift my husband gave me last night. He's gonna take me on a marriage retreat in April. Lillian wanted to know what we do on such weekends, and I told her about the singing. That song is one of my favorites. We sang it at our Lutheran church up in the Finger Lakes and it often is requested during the retreats, especially during the closing service."

"Yeah, me and my wife, we from AME Zion church down in Louisiana. But enough of us come here that we done started singing it at our Baptist Church over on South Benson Street."

"Hmm, "Lillian interjects, "Let me write down the name of that retreat you go to, Virginia. We gotta get back to work, soon. Nah!" she says swatting Ralph's hand when he reaches for the brochure.

Lillian pulls out her cell phone and clicks to her camera feature. "I'll just take a picture of the cover and check this out when I get home. I don't know if Louis is up to this right now. You know we had that weekend away last Fall when he got that award. It was a little strained, but we made it."

Ralph, too, is gathering up his lunch leftovers, overhears Lillian and comments,

"Yeah. We guys is so proud of Louis getting that national award for being a good supervisor. He real good to the teams of security, janitorial and gardening folks that nobody was surprised when we learned that group know about him, too. We famous now, 'cause we got a famous boss!" By this time, Ralph, talking loudly, is walking to the recycling bins.

Others in the café nod their heads when they hear Ralph praise the building supervisor. Ralph, smiling at the nods, nearly bumps into the square edge of the disposal bin with the flat tops on each side for stacking their trays once they put leftovers in the right bins for recycling or disposal.

Virginia finishes her drink, glances at the large wall clock and grabs her purse, her blond ponytail flipping from side to side. "Come on, Lillian. 'Bout time for us to be getting back to the office. I hope you and Louis decide to come this year. It's going to be at one of those resorts on the lake, just an hour or so away. So, you won't have to spend much on gas."

"Girl, quit it. We're not that cheap. We're just careful." Lillian slips her cell phone into her purse and hands the brochure back to Virginia. Once she's done a little more research, prayed and considered the implications of such a weekend, she'll bring up the idea with Louis. But she will order a packet, just in case. She still is old fashioned enough to prefer print to electronic stuff to read.

As the two women wash their hands in the Ladies' Room, Virginia tells Lillian that the Bible verse that goes with the theme this year is one she memorized in high school, and she quotes it while the two dry their hands.

"For I know the plans I have for you," declares the Lord,"

Lillian joins at the second line,

> *"plans to prosper you and not to harm you,*
> *plans to give you hope and a future. Then*
> *you will call on me and come and pray to*
> *Me, and I will listen to you. You will seek*
> *Me and find Me when you seek Me with all*
> *your heart.* (Jeremiah 29:11-13, NIV)

"Isn't it amazing how many of the same passages different congregations have their teens learn. Glennie and I learned that one in our high school Sunday School class and my teens have been asked to memorize those verses, too. Hmmm. This Agape Marriage group is sounding more and more attractive."

"And Lillian, this retreat is both interdenominational and interracial. I've been to Beth-El for your two weddings … to the same man!" she teases. "The gatherings will look a lot like that. You'll feel right at home."

Lillian gives her boss a gentle elbow bump and the two pick up their purses and head back to their respective offices.

As she settles down to work on the accounting files for the rest of the afternoon, Lilian muses. Thankfully, their kids are teens now and her sister, Glendella lives upstairs. Lillian and Louis have been blessed their entire married life to have trusted baby-sitters like Claude and Glendella who readily step in when needed. Having no extended biological family in the area has not proven a downside of either spouse since they moved here right out of college.

Virginia's Valentine's gift from her husband has made her really happy, her pale cheeks are nearly as red as the heart on the front of her card! The whole idea has given Lillian much to think about, but now she needs to get back to work. This job she's got today is a special contract, like those she sometimes picks up along the way. It can be reserved to help pay expenses if they choose to go on the marriage couples' retreat. Extra contract projects like this are paid in addition to her salary.

******

Once Lillian gets home, she is still wired about the possibility of the retreat, so she takes her laptop into the kitchen with her that evening. Once the meatloaf she'd fixed last night is reheating in the oven and the potatoes are cooking on the back eye, she pours frozen green peas into a small kettle and sets them on the front eye to cook a little later.

The Robertsons like their peas bright green and a little crunchy rather than greenish grey and mushy. So, she often just microwaves them for three or four minutes. Today, she'll just boil them briefly before seasoning them with spices to give them a little kick.

Once everything is set out for dinner, Lillian powers up the laptop. She searches to learn more about the elucidated purposes of marriage retreats, particularly those here in their state. She scrolls around to see some of the themes and activities one could expect during a weekend with people she doesn't know.

Ah, icebreakers at the opening session! She scans another page. Hmmm. The themes vary from site to site including plays on words like GPS "God's Plan for Success" to "Affirmations: Speaking Well of Ones' Spouse" and lots of the themes this year have to do with communication, like "Fighting Fair and Forgiving Quickly". Hmm. That's where Lillian and Louis are now.

Living beyond forgiveness, communicating honestly, and forgiving. Wow! This retreat idea may be worth the investment. What? What's that one? "Living in Synch: Raising Children Together". Well, with so many folks coming year after year, there are likely to be attendees with teens. Maybe she can ask others how they manage kids with such different personalities.

The buzzer on the oven rings before Lillian completes her research, so she tags the page and closes the laptop knowing she'll have to get back on this soon. She noticed that many of the retreats in her state have early registration dates and with just a couple months to go, she and Louis would have to decide if this is the year to go. Their son is graduating from high school. One down, two to go! Is this the time for Louis and me? Hmmm.

An Anchor or A Buoy?

Sylvester Cedric Jackson, Pastor of Beth-El Community Church, and his wife have been attending an online married couples' group for the past year, a gathering offered by the ministers in their state. Originally the umbrella group was organized for pastors to meet in much the same way that practicing psychologists and psychiatrists are required to meet to maintain their certification. It is a professional standard for psychotherapists to have their own therapists and to meet regularly in order to unwind in confidence and to stay up to date on the research regarding their practice.

Five years ago, when Pastor Jackson had completed his academic studies at the seminary, he and his cohort were encouraged to join and maintain a relationship with experienced clergy to nurture their spiritual and personal growth. There was another Sylvester in the group, so he has begun using his middle name, Cedric. His wife had preferred that name. Now that's what he uses … most of the time.

This group also has meetings for pastor's spouses, and biannually, a weekend for couples. It is their regular attendance to both support groups that enable Cedric and Kamia, his wife, to hang in there when the demands of pastoring seem overwhelming. They are encouraged to support one another with the Word. It was their recommendation of this online site that inspired Louis and Lillian to continue trusted counseling in this more affordable way.

The hosts of the online group do not require confessions. Instead, the facilitators offer short Bible-based presentations, then time for couples to write for about ten to twelve minutes their responses to thought-provoking prompts. When the buzzer rings, they are instructed to turn and discuss the topic of the day privately with their spouse. After ten minutes or so, participants in the session return for closing time together where they can verbalize questions for clarification, before closing in prayer.

It is the structured focus and guiding questions that help most couples face the truth of their attitudes and behaviors and together commit to allowing the Holy Spirit to help them release, forgive, and move on.

Since the spouses committed to be honest with one another, even if it makes them look bad themselves, some weeks can be joyous and others a disappointment. Still, this regular time to reflect on the past week and to consider ways they had and could use the Word to guide them provides just the impetus Cedric and Kamia need to grow in the Lord.

******

This final week in March, the group leader lets the words of the hymn "The Solid Rock" serve as his teaching tool. The leader opens in prayer, and then simply shares his screen with the words showing and the accompaniment playing. He invites those attending to mute their microphones and to sing along, paying close attention to the fact that this song, sung in the first-person point of view, is a confessional hymn.

> My hope is built on nothing less
> than Jesus' blood and righteousness;
> I dare not trust the sweetest frame,
> but wholly lean on Jesus' name.
>
> Refrain:
>
> On Christ, the solid Rock, I stand:
> all other ground is sinking sand;
> all other ground is sinking sand.

When darkness veils his lovely face,
I rest on his unchanging grace;
in every high and stormy gale,
my anchor holds within the veil.

Once the song ends, the lesson of the week takes an unexpected turn. Instead of asking the participants, as he's done in other lessons, to choose a verse of the hymn and write about it, the leader asks, "Which is true for you? Has Christ been an anchor or a buoy for you this week? For those of you who don't recall, according to the Merriam-Webster dictionary, an anchor is a device usually of metal attached to a ship or boat by a cable and cast overboard to hold it in a particular place by means of a fluke that digs into the bottom."

He stops, knowing some in attendance are familiar with "fluke" as a slang term meaning "accidental" or "freakish" and wonder why such a term would be used in a Bible study.

The leader moves quickly to define that in this case, a fluke is a triangular metal piece at the end of an anchor that digs into the ground to hold it in place.

"Ah ha!" Cedric says aloud to Kamia. "He's talking about the Trinity, the Father, Son, and Holy Spirit. You think?" Kamia nods but returns her attention to the online speaker.

"Or," the leader continues, "has Christ been a buoy for you this week? Now those who are unfamiliar with these seaside terms, let me explain. A buoy is a floating marker set up to let ships, boats, and swimmers know when it is safe to move on."

"Hmm." Cedric puzzles aloud. "An anchor to hold me in place? I thought we're supposed to be growing in the Lord, not standing stagnant."

"Hon, will you just listen?" Kamia admonishes kindly. "You know he's going somewhere with this."

The leader clarifies by projecting this saying on the screen. As he reads aloud Kamia gasps. She'd seen the same motivational post on Facebook just a couple of days ago. "If you don't let the past die, it won't let you live." She swallows and leans forward attentively, listening to the leader.

"My dear brothers and sisters, Christ our Savior can be both a buoy for us and an anchor. When we get into troubled water, issues in the past seem to tumble through our minds, like Hurricane Katrina! We need markers to let us know when it is safe to move on. In such times, we need an anchor to hold us secure until we see the path to safety.

"I'm going to play the song again and ask you to copy in your journal a phrase that speaks to you this week. Then, for the rest of the time, write about a past issue that hasn't seemed to die, yet. Acknowledge that issue and ways its presence is blocking or contaminating your relationship with your spouse.

"Is there something you need to confess or forgive? Have you confessed and forgiven, but not allowed the issue to die? Be honest. Do what must be done so you can move on as a couple prepared to support each other in the ministries the Lord has in mind for you in your home, your church, or your community."

He pauses a moment to allow time for the couples who've joined this week to contemplate the challenge he's set out for them. Then he goes on.

"From where you are, look out the window. You likely see evidence of buds returning to trees that have been dormant all winter. Consider this a metaphor for this time of your marriage. If it's a leaf that has not yet fallen, release it so a new bud can grow and blossom this Spring and Summer."

He then reshares his screen so the lyrics of the song, "The Solid Rock" are on view. The participants in the virtual audience hear the mixed-gender choir singing the song dramatically. The couples viewing and listening concentrate on the lyrics.

> His oath, his covenant, his blood,
> support me in the whelming flood;
> when all around my soul gives way,
> he then is all my hope and stay.
>
> When he shall come with trumpet sound,
> O may I then in him be found:
> dressed in his righteousness alone,
> faultless to stand before the throne.

Suddenly, Cedric recalls from his conversations with Lillian and Louis that in their work with the marriage counselor, Dr. Manguel highlighted that admitting, confessing, and forgiving are among the first steps along the journey of reconciliation. This couple is in their second lap around, having vowed in that public ceremony at the church to remain married and to allow the Lord to heal the hurts they've experienced as a couple due to Louis' orientation as a bisexual man. Louis had lost his lover and Lillian had lost her trust in her husband.

Cedric knows they've forgiven each other, but both feel the issues are not yet all dead. They want to live together but are frustrated when either one makes a statement alluding to something "back in the day" before the Reveal. They've mentioned in a counseling session last Fall, that they've have been advised to follow Apostle Paul's advice written to the Corinthians, to resume having physical marital relations. They both are healthy and may now experience the physical releases. He doubts that it's been an easy move in their marriage.

Louis probably wonders, does she know that I love her and am with her one hundred percent?

Lillian probably wonders, does he wish he were with Claude instead of with me?

Thinking of them, as their brother in the Lord, Cedric, decides to share the program link with Louis and Lillian and sends it to them right away. He knows this is their evening time together so is not surprised when Louis replies, "Got it! Looks provocative, but we'll view it tomorrow evening."

******

The next evening, the Robertsons do just that. They both have been reluctant to verbalize these feelings. This evening, once they have their thoughts on paper, and the soft timer rings, instead of speaking aloud, they just exchange journals. As each reads the other's writing, they breathe a sigh of relief. Thank God, it's out. He knows. She knows. Ah, Jesus is both a Buoy and the Anchor.

Louis passes Lillian's journal back to her, and signals with a nod to set it on the narrow table between their chairs. She does and he takes her hand, gently squeezes it, and says, "Sweetie. What I wrote is the truth. I do love you and yes, I do think of Claude sometimes. But not in that way anymore. The desire for a physical relationship with him is dimming significantly since I prayed that prayer for release. I'll always love him as a friend and brother, but no longer as a lover. You are all I need and want."

Lillian, a little damp-eyed, reaches for a tissue from a box on the shelf under their side table, wipes her eyes and nose, and admits, "I'm learning to love you, too, Louie. And I find that I'm less distracted by thoughts of you and Claude, but I admit, the images do arise. I'm confident that is Satan bringing up scenes to stifle the confidence I seem to have lost when I learned about the length of your relationship with Claude and the fact that I never even suspected."

"Well, there, my dear, we can say 'Thank the Lord.' Crazy as it seems, I'm glad you have not been uncomfortable with our marriage all this time and only staying because of the kids. We have been happy as a family, and I believe it's because I have been faithful to you the way I understood it at the time. As mentioned before, being bisexual, I thought it fine to be monogamous with each of my partners. But, again, thank the Lord, when Claude and I learned that it is not Biblical to be in an intimate physical relationship with anyone other than one's spouse, we knew we had to stop."

"And …," Lillian goes on, now that the topic is in the open, "a triple, thank the Lord. The Holy Spirit convinced Claude to follow the sacrificial model of the Lord and to remove himself as a temptation so that our Robertson family could remain whole. Isn't it weird that we had to tear apart to become whole? God certainly is something else!" Louis squeezes her hand, gently signifying agreement.

"Yes …! Oh Louis!" Lillian yelps. "It's time to rejoin the program. Our leader is back. What's he going to be saying now?"

The two return their attention to the marriage counseling program. The leader has opened the floor for questions, but there are none during this segment. This confessional journal writing has quieted the dozen or so couples who've been meeting for this series. Cautious about publicizing their personal issues, none seems to be in a place to verbalize a question. In fact, most turned off their cameras and he can only see their screen names.

So, the virtual group leader moves on and participants click their cameras on again. He refers them to several verses in Romans that remind them that Christians are accountable for what they know. And then this well-read minister paraphrases a quotation by Maya Angelou, "I did then what I knew how to do. Now that I know better, I do better." and then, he closes in prayer and plays the opening hymn one more time.

His oath, his covenant, his blood,
support me in the whelming flood;
when all around my soul gives way,
he then is all my hope and stay.

The group leader watches his screen, noting that the couples listen and nod. He prays that the three points made today make this song more poignant. He's told them about buoys and anchors, that each person must let the past die in order to live today, and that each is accountable for behaving based on what they now know.

On Christ, the solid Rock, I stand:
all other ground is sinking sand;
all other ground is sinking sand.

Lillian and Louis now give thanks to the Lord as each notices the softening of earlier stiff shoulders and the start of gentle smiles. They both begin singing confidently, confessing that the Word can be the buoy and Jesus Christ, the Anchor because He is the Solid Rock. This Scripture is one that keeps them going. They know the Apostle Paul is writing to one of the churches he helped to plant in Philippi, but this contemporary couple feel it speaks to them, too.

I thank my God every time I remember you.
In all my prayers for all of you, I always
pray with joy because of your partnership in
the gospel from the first day until now, being
confident of this, that he who began a good
work in you will carry it on to completion
until the day of Christ Jesus. (Philippians
1:3-7, NIV)

What Dr. Manguel had counseled about the value of letting go is beginning to make more sense as Louis and Lillian each grows more confident, trusting that God is healing them of the past and preparing them for the future.

Spring Choices

What's Upsetting Her?

Alysa yelps! Lillian nearly drops the tongs when she hears her daughter screeching. Recouping, this startled mother slaps this stainless-steel cooking utensil on a square cotton potholder sitting in the metal center of the stovetop. Turning meat for dinner will have to wait! Lillian flicks the stove dial to off and dashes into her daughter's bedroom. Her youngest child lies flailing on the floor! Fists punch the air. Feet pound the rug next to her bed. She is rolling from side to side as though she's trying to kick someone or something off the top of her.

"Lysa, Lysa, Lysa," the alarmed mother cries, kneeling next to her sixteen-year-old daughter, now panting as though she has run a marathon. "What's the matter, Baby? Mommy's here!"

"Get him off!" Alysa shrieks. "Get him off of me!" she cries, whipping her fists from left to right. Her eyes bulge, glazed from the tears welling up in her bronze, brown eyes.

"Get who off?" Lillian's eyes dart, looking behind her and in the corner. "I don't see anyone!" By this time, Alysa has stopped trembling, but now turns onto her side, pulling her knees up into the fetal position.

"Mom! How'd you do it? How'd you get him to leave me alone?"

Still on the floor next to her daughter, Lillian gathers Alysa into her arms, not from the front, but from the back and cradles as best she can this teenage girl nearly as tall as her mom. "Honey, tell me what happened. Who did you see?"

Alysa relaxes a little in her mother's embrace and says nothing.

Lillian asks again, "Who did you see?"

"I don't know, Mommy. I was reading my Sunday School lesson tonight 'cause Sister Lizabeth asked me to create some slides to go with the lesson next week."

"Yes, and…what is that lesson about that got you so upset."

"It was from Matthew 4 about Jesus being tested in the wilderness by Satan. I was trying to visualize what it must have looked like so I could create slides to go with the lesson."

"You've got quite an imagination, Lysa, but this is a little over the top! Which verses got you so upset?"

Her daughter shakes her head.

"Come on, Lysa." She squeezes her daughter a bit. "Let's pray first, then read these verses together." By this time her daughter has relaxed some, still amazed that her mind could take her to such a fearful place that she reacted so emotionally and physically.

"Sure, Mom. Sorry about getting you so startled. I have no idea what happened, but I know that I was frightened out of my wits. So glad you were home early today!" Alyssa sighs, leaning into her mom's warm arms.

"Yeah, me, too, Lysa. Virginia told us we may as well go home 'cause we're probably gonna have to work late next week. It's nearly time for the quarterly reports and all the paperwork is not in from the stores in our chain. We can't do the computation for them yet."

Then, feeling Alysa recompose herself and getting up, Lillian says a little more casually, but with equal gratefulness. "Well, we never know why the Lord works things out the way He does. I certainly would not have wanted you home alone having this vision or with just you and Lou. He would have freaked out, for sure."

"Well, Mom. Come over here. Look at this." Alysa turns her laptop screen so Lillian can see as she looks over her daughter's shoulder.

"Lysa!" Shocked at what she sees on the screen, Lillian says tapping her daughter's elbow, "Let's take the laptop into the living room. We can sit on the sofa and go over this together. There's something going on here and with the help of the Lord, we can get to the bottom of this lesson and your response to it."

"Okay, Mom. Let me bring my Sunday School book, too. I gotta see where this lesson's supposed to be going. Sometimes I can get an idea when I look at the questions at the end."

"Good thinking," Lillian says, putting her arm around Alysa as they walk slowly to the living room. They push the coffee table out from the sofa before sitting there, hips touching so their physical connection remains as they attempt to make the mental connection between reading the Word and flailing on the floor.

Alysa keys in the words to locate that passage from Matthew on one of the Bible websites, and as the two await the page to show up, she turns to her mother and pleads, "Mom, you're not going to tell Dad, are you?"

"I should, but I think it'll be better if you do that yourself. But now, let's look at this passage." The picture she'd seen on her daughter's screen resembled what Lillian had seen on Alysa's face when she walked into the room. In the drawing is a character shown flat but flailing on the floor with a fantasy cartoony-looking monster holding the person down by the shoulders. It is not clear whether the person is male or female. It didn't matter; the look on the face is utter fright!

The mother and daughter read aloud the verses from the Gospel of Matthew, describing how Jesus being very hungry, is visited by the "tempter" who entices him three times to do something forbidden by the Law. Lillian still tries to figure out why such a reading would upset her daughter so much.

Then, at the end of the Sunday School lesson text, she sees a sentence that may have triggered such a reaction to her daughter now in her transition years. She's a relatively new Christian who is just beginning to take the veracity and timeliness of Scripture seriously. And, as an artist, her daughter is known to be able to visualize and sketch what she sees in her mind.

Later that evening, sitting at the dinner table, Lillian looks at Alysa and nods toward Louis, signaling her daughter to tell her father what had happened that afternoon. Alysa shakes her head and mouths, "Not now."

Louis notices the silent communication between his wife and daughter and asks, "Okay. You, two," he says looking from left to right. "What's up? You've been acting odd all evening."

"Yeah," Lou Jr. adds, "Something's going on. You may as well tell us. Remember," he adds philosophically, "we promised to be truth-tellers. Sometimes saying nothing is as much a lie as verbalizing an untruth."

Alysa wiggles her shoulders and takes a deep breath. "Okay!" Then she exhales. "I had a fit this afternoon."

"What do you mean a fit?" inquiring Louis asks. "Lillian, will you explain? Lysa is looking uncomfortable."

"Well," Lillian replies after taking a deep pull on her glass of ice water. "It seems like Alysa had a wrestle with the Devil."

"A wrestle with the Devil! Lysa, what's Mom talking about?"

Alysa, raises her head, looks around the table, and nods to her mother. Lillian then describes what had occurred when she went into the room and saw her daughter writhing on her bedroom floor as though she was losing a battle with an invisible beast.

Lou is the first to ask his sister, "Lysa, what brought this on?"

Now that she's heard the story again, her demeaner less stressed, Alysa explains, "I'd just read the Bible story about Jesus being confronted by Satan and I wanted to know what that looked like. So, I lay down on the floor, closed my eyes and unwittingly invited the experience to become real for me.

"Before I knew it, I felt a weight on me and pressure on my shoulders. When I swatted and wiggled, I didn't feel anything. That scared me so I called for Mom. Thank God, she was home early from work!" Alysa reaches across the table and touches her mom's hand, even though it is still encircling the water glass. "Thanks, Mom."

Louis shakes his head in disbelief. "Lysa, I know you have an active imagination. But this is truly weird. We read about stories of Satanic attacks, but I never expected one to occur in my own home!" He slams his hand on the table. "How did that spirit get through with as much prayer as goes on here?"

"Good question, Dad," Lou Jr. affirms. "But, when you think about it, Satan got to Jesus," their thoughtful, maturing son espouses. "Jesus told his disciples to expect similar experiences, but not to fear them. Like Him, we have the Word and the Holy Spirit."

Reaching to pat his son on the shoulder, Louis encourages, "You're right there, Sonny. Thank the Lord for the Word and for the prayer, and for you, Sweetie," he says reaching for Lillian's hand. "I can't imagine what this evening would have been like if you'd not been home!"

******

That Sunday, Sister Elizabeth, the Sunday School teacher, explains, "Just as Eve was tempted and gave in, you, too will be tempted to do things that are not right for you. Sometimes, it will be simple things like ingesting or inhaling something that is not healthy. Sometimes, it may be doing physically dangerous things like giving into the dares in gym, at the swimming pool, or out hiking in the woods, and sometimes it will be temptations to do or say things to make you seem wiser or better than anyone else."

Nearly the whole group of teens seated around the two eight-foot tables leans in to see the slides Alyssa created, then lean back, many with wrinkled eyebrows. When their teacher continues, most listen attentively.

"Eve gave in," their teacher continues, "but, Jesus, though in His human body, did not. What did he use to shield himself from Satan's temptations?"

The teens respond en masse, "He quoted the Scriptures." She nods and smiles. Something is getting through to them. That's why this Sunday School teacher encourages the teens in her class to go beyond knowing the stories, and on to memorizing the Scriptures. They never know when such knowledge will be all they would have to stand between them and a tempter.

Equally important, during that Sunday School lesson on the Temptations of Christ, she reiterated to the high schoolers that being a Christian did not mean they would never be tempted. Jesus was. Be ready as He was. Being Christians did not mean they would never give in to some temptations. Be ready, for the gift of God's mercy. God forgives confessed sin, and she urges them to keep that in mind. God is merciful and with open arms accepts back into the fold those who have strayed.

Then, though it is not in the Sunday School book, Brother Melvin, their co-teacher, has them turn to Galatians 6:1-5. He invites Amarion, one of their more expressive readers, to read it aloud.

Brothers and sisters, if someone is caught in
a sin, you who live by the Spirit should
restore that person gently. But watch
yourselves, or you also may be tempted.
Carry each other's burdens, and in this way
you will fulfill the law of Christ. If anyone
thinks they are something when they are not,
they deceive themselves. Each one should
test their own actions. Then they can take
pride in themselves alone, without
comparing themselves to someone else, for
each one should carry their own load.
(Galatians 6:1-5, NIV)

Patrick, one of the young men who seldom speaks in class, raises his hand and, when signaled to speak, verbalizes his observation,

"Isn't that contradictory? Who are we to compare ourselves to if not to someone who is living for the Lord?"

The co-teacher responds firmly, "To Christ and Christ alone! He is the person in the Bible we know who came to the aid of those who needed help and has no sin recorded about him."

"Well, Brother Melvin. If we can't be perfect, why compare ourselves to the Perfect One?"

"Hmmm. Good questions, Patrick. I'm not sure how to answer that, but I can say, that when we can, we should help restore others to the fold. We should remind them that God loves them and when they confess their sins, He will forgive them.

"This passage of Scripture from Paul, urges us to be there for each other." This co-teacher quickly sits back in his chair when Sister Elizabeth indicates that time is up for the day. He's glad to be off the hot seat!

She closes the lesson that Sunday with the teens reading or reciting "The Lord's Prayer" which summarizes in Christ's own words the facts of being tempted and forgiven.

******

Later that week, Alysa sits at the picnic table in the backyard as she awaits the wooden jewelry to absorb the mix Uncle Claude told her would make the balsa wood more pliable. In her head, she recites a poem she had drafted. Even when it's not April Poetry Month, her English teacher regularly challenges them to draft poems based on prompts she gets from one of those online teacher groups.

One morning, the teacher asked them to close their eyes and think of something in nature they'd seen and about ways that scene in nature linked to something they had experienced emotionally. Alysa had written,

> A blue bird scampers across the green grass
> Chirping and singing with sass
> Pausing to peak as though it were hiding in plain view
> Just like I used to do.
>
> The thorns on the roses protect it
> Like I hoped my cool words would do
> When I was having a temper fit.
> When they wouldn't include me, too.

Just this morning, her mom had her youngest daughter stay in the kitchen with her to help clear up after breakfast. In their chat, she raised the fact that Alysa seems to be losing her temper more these days and wonders precisely what's causing this change in temperament.

Mother admitted to Alysa that seeing her in the fit she had had last week, flailing around on her bedroom floor, had nearly made her call the school counselor. She acknowledged to her daughter that she understands the young ones are alert to similar ups and downs in their parents' lives, who have their own on and off days, too.

Yes, this concerned mom had verbalized, she and her husband have committed their hearts and marriage to the Lord. Yes, they have faith that He will give them the strength to continue along the path to maturity, but neither is there yet. She promised her daughter that she'd try to be more open with the fact that believers often struggle to put into practice the Word they are taught, read, and meditate on.

Alysa glances over to the back of the house and sees her mom is watching her from the window. The daughter flicks a small wave and goes back to thinking about why she feels so left out. It seems everyone in the family has something special going on, but her.

Yes, she continues to do her jewelry making, but it's not nearly as much fun doing it alone. She had been accustomed to challenges from her sister about who could finish their new piece soonest. Of course, it was her artwork, and for Alvyra, learning a new section of her clarinet solo. Now, she's gone.

Once they moved to this new house, the twins no longer shared a bedroom, but they usually spent some time together in one room or the other each evening.

No more of that. In fact, Alysa stopped going into Alvyra's room once she learned her mother had been sleeping there instead of in bed with her husband. Lou Jr. had told Aunt Glendella that he could hear their mom tipping into the room once she thought the teens were asleep. Apparently, she'd forgotten that his basement bedroom is right under Alvyra's room. Oh well. Can't hide much around here.

While Alysa is feeling out of it, she is not sure what her family is doing that she wants to be more a part of now. Maybe it's something else she's alluding to in her poem. True, Jabari has asked her to be his date for the Senior Ball. But … she rationalizes … that's just probably because of her brother.

She has noticed they've become better friends and spending more time together. Because, quiet as is kept, she finds she enjoys being with Jabari and wonders if she's curiously jealous. He seems to respect her in ways that keep his hands to himself. She hopes it's not because he and her brother, like her dad, are gay.

In the side yard, below the juniper trees that separate their yard from Ms. Andrea's, Alysa notices the blooming daffodils. The rich yellows are making her smile. Maybe she'll try mixing paints for the necklace she is making. Uncle Claude taught her that adding white to primary colors can make them appear brighter. Maybe that is what she needs today.

The sun is shining, but it's been a grayish yellow portending possible rain. Alysa knows rain is needed for Spring flowers to blossom, but she's not ready for rain now. On the other hand, after the rain one often can spot a rainbow.

Hmmm. Maybe she'll make a rainbow-colored necklace. Mixing those different colors so each shines brightly may provide just the reminder a future customer needs to buy a gift for a family or friend who has down days like she's having today.

Alysa jumps when the buzzer on her cellphone alarm rings, and nearly tips over the barbecue grill her dad has pulled out of storage, but not yet cleaned up for cooking this season. She steadies the dome-topped monstrosity and walks briskly to the wood shop in the garage.

Strange as it seems, the warmth of the sun is cooling her down. She doesn't feel as restless as described in the poem she'd written in school, or she recalled in the conversation with her mother. She doesn't even think her temper will erupt if anyone says anything to her about the link between the queer community and rainbow colors. That group probably chose the rainbow to give thanks to God who creates diversity as seen in flora and fauna, birds and beasts, the fish of the sea, and in humans, too.

What's Exciting Her?

Alvyra obviously is all wound up about something. She bounces in her chair as the family logs on for their Sunday Zoom meeting. She usually logs on from the bedroom she shares with Valerie, the teenage daughter of Alvyra's host family there in France.

"You're mighty wiggly tonight, Vyra," Lillian says once the family is all logged on and she can see their faces in the little boxes on her screen. They each login on their own devices so they can sit back and chat for fifteen or twenty minutes during this semi-monthly online meeting with Vyra. Only one family rule. "Each must keep their camera on." It's seeing as well as hearing that makes the time together so special.

They often gather in the front room, each with their own laptop, tablet, or phone. This week, however, Lou Jr. is downstairs, but he's online. Alyssa is seated at the dining room table, 'cause she's also trying to finish an assignment for school tomorrow. It's late evening for Alvyra, so they try to keep that in mind.

"Well, Mom and Dad! You know that Valerie, my French sister is taking English to fulfill her World Language requirement at our school. In fact, that's one of the reasons her parents consented to board me. I can help their daughter with her English, and she can help me with my French. Anyway, let me hurry and tell you what happened last week."

Alyssa leans in a bit; she's both curious and jealous. Alvyra gets this special full family attention twice a month. The family seems to just be watching Alyssa, but seldom actually ask her how she's doing. That startling fit on her bedroom floor still has the family on edge. It was just an artistic exploration. Scary, but something that just happened. She's over that.

Alvyra, once she sees she has everyone's attention, goes on to explain that each of the students in World Language classes must do a presentation based on a cultural event celebrated in a country in which the language being studied is the dominant language. Valerie chose the United States, and her event was Black History Month. She had learned that James Weldon Johnson wrote "Lift Every Voice and Sing" for kids to present at a program celebrating Abraham Lincoln and that song became known as the Negro National Anthem, now called the Black National Anthem.

"Anyway, Valerie learned the lyrics and because she's a singer, on the day she gave her report, she invited me to come accompany her on my clarinet. She sang the first verse, I played the second verse while the lyrics were projected on the class whiteboard, and then as she sang the third verse, I played the alto line. We'd been using YouTube video while we practiced, so we were lit when we did that song. Oh Mom, you woulda been so proud."

"Wow!" her mother commends! " I imagine I would have been. You're really a talented musician!"

"And…guess what? The teacher taped us. See, I just uploaded the video in the chat. You can watch it when we get offline tonight."

"Girl, it's afternoon here!" Lou Jr., quips. "Yeah, I saw the link That's really cool. I downloaded the file. We'll watch this evening."

"And…" Alvyra continues. "You know what, Lysa?"

"What else?" Alysa asks dryly, a little moody because her twin is dominating the conversation this week.

"Valerie wore the necklace you made for her. She included that in her report."

"What you mean, in her report?" Alyssa asks, not sure if this will be a positive or negative addition to her twin's story.

"Well," Alvyra continues, "she showed it when she talked about enslaved persons carrying on their artwork once they got to the States and many of the grandmothers passed along those skills to their progeny. Yeah, she said, 'progeny'. You can imagine how surprised she was when I told her you learned that skill from a White man of European descent!"

The Robertsons chuckle as the oldest twin winds up her report for happenings there in France.

"Her comeback was, well, they always say the United States is a melting pot. You know I called her on that one right away! I told her 'We ain't melting! We're a mosaic, each of us retaining what is unique and special and sharing with those who wish to learn!"

"Ah, listen to the D.I.E. professor!" Lou Jr. teases. " You sound like one of those diversity, inclusion, and equity speakers we had at the high school a couple of weeks ago!"

Lillian hears the faint buzz of the timer she sets for these gatherings and nods to Lou to take the lead.

"Well, Honey. Sounds like you had a wonderful celebration of Black History Month on many levels. We'll watch and pray that your stay continues to be one where you can share as much as you learn. Let's pray."

"Wait a minute, Daddy. One more thing! I learned my name, Alvyra, means "foreign" and here I am studying abroad in a foreign country! Mom, how'd you know that would be my road in life?"

"I didn't. God did," she chuckles and noticing the time, she says, "Remember the rule, everybody, touch your screen and raise your hand." She begins singing their benediction song, "God Be with You Till We Meet Again." None in the family is concerned anymore that singing online means they're not totally in touch. That's life.

God be with you till we meet again;
loving counsels guide, uphold you,
may the Shepherd's care enfold you;
God be with you till we meet again.

But they all do stop at the refrain. They no longer sing that during gatherings like this because the lyrics make Alysa uncomfortable.

Till we meet, till we meet,
till we meet at Jesus' feet.
Till we meet, till we meet,
God be with you till we meet again.

They had discovered that when they got to the line "meet at Jesus' feet" Alysa thought the family was singing that song because one of them may die instead of returning. So, mindful of Alysa's active imagination, they just repeat the last line of the first verse a little slower. In family, "me" is not the most important person there. They show they care and the emotions they spare.

And, as one can imagine, Alysa quickly looks up the meaning of her name! Is she ever surprised!

Think He'll Do It?

The Beth-El men's baseball team is gearing up to compete this season and James Milton decides to invite Glendella to come to the afternoon practice game and have a light dinner with him afterward. He'd learned over time, that she likes international cuisines and so decided to take her to the new Thai restaurant that had recently opened in the next town. The short drive would be an opportunity to get to know one another a little better. But for safety's sake, he has decided to make this a double date. So, James invited Paul and his wife, Marlene, to join them. They consented.

******

"Well, Guys," Paul says as he clicks his seatbelt into place and takes his wife's hand. "We've no place to go but up."

"True, there, Bro," James confirms. "We played pretty well though. Louis nearly caught that ball in center field. We're not as fleet a foot as we'll be later in the season. And, we had a great cheering squad on the sidelines."

"Yeah," Paul's wife, Marlene says. "I hope the seats are cleaned by the opening game. I just couldn't sit on all that grime knowing we'd be going out to dinner afterward."

"Me neither," Glendella adds, turning a bit in her front seat so she can see one of the two sitting behind her. "But, it really was an exciting game to watch. No one would believe so many old men could hit, run, and catch enough to score as many runs as they both scored this time."

"It was the pitching that was so good," James reflects. "I think those guys forgot they were pitching against their opponents. Nearly every pitch sailed right across the plate about mid-waist. None of us had problems hitting. It was getting around those bases in time that got us." Very soon, they're at the street where he can turn right and merge onto the expressway that will get them to the next town in ten minutes or so.

"Phil nearly got that tie homerun when he tried to slide in. Too bad he slid by the base rather than into it." They all chuckle. Glad to be together, healthy enough to play and to watch and cheer.

As they drive into the restaurant parking lot, Paul suggests, "How about we each get a different dish and share them? You know, sort a smorgasbord like."

"Sure." replies Glendella.

"Why not?" asks Marlene.

"Sounds like a plan to me." agrees James, as he parks in a slot just a few steps from the entry to the restaurant. The menu is posted on the window where passersby can view before entering. That's convenient, so the four of them stand, look, read, and plan what to order.

"Well, folks, what're you going to get?" asks Glendella, the organizer. "Let's try to get a variety to try different spices. Only thing is, I don't eat pork. So, if any of you gets Pad Kra Pao Moo with that minced pork stir-fried with chili and thai basil, I'll pass." All nod, and walk inside as James, in his usher mode, holds open the door for the women to enter first.

The restaurant hostess dressed in Thai attire with a long skirt, and a top that ties to the side, greets them in Thai that sounded like "Yindi bondiot", then says, "Welcome" in English. James nods pleased that the owners are retaining their cultural language and acknowledging that their new customers may be unfamiliar with it, so the waiters and waitresses hired are bilingual.

Hearing the language and music in the background while inhaling the tantalizing aroma, and then consuming the cuisine with a variety of herbs, spices, and textures gives clients quite an authentic experience.

The four adults savor the delicacies, talk and just enjoy their time together. The waiter honors their request to share each item and brings appropriate small bowls or plates for each person. The diners begin with Tom Kha Gai, coconut soup with chicken. For entrees, they share Khao Pad, fried rice with chicken; Pad Thai, Thai fried noodles; and Gai Pad Med Ma Muang, stir-fried chicken with cashew nuts, before a dessert of Kluay Kaek, thai fritters, and hardy cups of coffee seasoned with cardamom.

So begins regular dating. This nearly fifty-year old pair, James and Glendella, often attend, as a couple, small group social events with friends like Paul and Marlene who watch with interest to see how this relationship is going.

As Glendella reflects on these past couple of months, she's glad she followed that Facebook post that said, "When I wanted to give up, God told me to get up." So, that's what she's been doing. Getting up each day, with eyes wide open to see where God is leading and how He will fulfill her dream to marry for love. Still, she's being vigilant.

******

It's been years, now. Since that time, long ago, Glendella has become exceptionally cautious about private conversations once she learned how a man she didn't even know, Quentin Rupert, had found out she was infertile. When she was in community college, she had arranged to meet with friends to work on a class project. They were to meet at a restaurant not far from her doctor's office downtown.

Unknown to her at the time, Quentin was a waiter there and had overheard her confessing that alarming doctor's revelation about her infertility. In fact, knowing she'd never be able to have children was one of the reasons he'd made that strange proposal of marriage all those years ago!

He exclaimed that she could help him stay a Christian, traveling with him and not being encumbered by childcare. She'd always wanted to travel and when neither of them had job prospects when they graduated, he joined the Air Force, and she joined him as his wife.

Now, this nearly fifty-year-old widow chooses to meet her new friend, James, at their local library. Over time, both have spilled facts about their relationships with their now-dead spouses. He honors Glendella's wish to be seen but not heard. She honors his unspoken wish to spend time together without having to spend money, but not meeting at either of their apartments.

He's a widowed man who feels attracted to and by Glendella. She's a widow-woman feeling physically drawn to this man. She's been watchful. James has displayed recognizable gestures that suggest arousal, too. Neither of them wants to jump the gun. So, many Saturday afternoons they just meet at the local library in hopes that one of the study rooms is available. Those little rooms with a small table, comfortable chairs, and large glass walls are just right for this kind of safe getting-to-know-you time. The couple have auditory privacy. but remain visible.

James who passionately loved his wife confesses to resenting God for taking her while pregnant with their third child. Both had died. It was James' mother who encouraged him to question God all he wanted, but not to lose his faith. He admits that was easier said than done, in those early years. But, with his family support and prayer, he eventually recommitted his life to God, accepted Christ's gift of love and the power of the Holy Spirit to help him control his sexual drive.

Glendella, on the other hand, admitted to never having that passionate relationship with her husband. It remained a satisfactory one once they learned and practiced the teaching they had in a Bible study for married couples. There they learned by reading,

> *The husband should fulfill his marital duty*
> *to his wife, and likewise the wife to her*
> *husband... Do not deprive each other except*
> *by mutual consent for a time, so that you*
> *may devote yourselves to prayer. Then come*
> *together again so that Satan will not tempt*
> *you because of your lack of self-control.*
> *(I Corinthians 7:3, 5, NIV)*

Their Bible study about marriage taught them that as long as they did not deny each other marital physical relations, they'd be fine. Her husband loved his work; she loved her music. As long as they remained faithful to God, He would give them the desires of their hearts as aligned with His Word.

******

Now, this Saturday in late March, Glendella gets a call from James.

"Morning, Glennie. Wanna meet at the library this afternoon?"

"Sure, you got some research to do? Want me to help?"

"Nah, not this time. Just gotta run some errands this morning and 'cause the weather's not all that warm today, I thought we could meet there and chat … about nothing in particular."

"Well, that certainly sounds exciting," Glendella replies with a smile. "But, yeah. Sure. I can finish what I'm doing and be there this afternoon. What time?"

"About one-ish. I should be through by then."

"Okay, and if I get there first, I'll sign up for one of those study rooms. We can't keep meeting and talking in the open space. Didn't you see the librarian giving us the eye the last time? I thought sure he was gonna come over and kick us out when we started laughing so loud."

"Yeah, you right. I remember that. Sure, let's try for one of those study rooms. If I get there first, I'll sign us up and wait for you upstairs in the fiction section over there by the windows overlooking that woodsy area. Those lilac trees are starting to blossom. I really like looking at those purply flowers and the grasses greening around them."

"Okay, James. See you about one o'clock."

Once settled in the center study room on the left side of the library, the two catch up on their week and then Glendella switches topics and exclaims with excitement,

"You know this is the first week of Lent?"

"Yes. Remember, I was at church Sunday, ushering in fact. Yes, I heard Pastor Jackson announce plans for special services each week. What's up? You and your sister gonna do a special musical piece one of those weeks?"

"No, I was thinking of something different for Palm Sunday and having the kids or teens march up the center aisle of the sanctuary waving palm fronds."

"Where'd you get an idea for something like that?"

Glendella goes on to describe a Palm Sunday service she experienced when she and her husband were stationed at Edwards Air Force Base in California. That Sunday morning, the kids in the primary class each had been given eight fronds of Robellini palm branches.

During the opening hymn the little ones had marched in waving the palms, then stopped, one pair of children at each row of pews in the sanctuary, then they handed the fronds to those seated in that row. An adult usher was there to hand out palms if there were more than eight folks seated there.

"Weren't those tree branches too heavy for kids that little?" Papa James asks imagining how his own children would have managed when they were that age.

"No, palms are not all that heavy. Even though most of them were twelve to twenty inches long." Glendella clarifies holding her hands apart to show the size of a typical palm branch used for this purpose.

"Well, okay. Then, what?" asks James.

"The music minister invited the congregants to wave the palms from left to right during the songs of praise and worship, then slip the palms under the seats in front of them until after the sermon."

Throwing his head back as though to visualize such a festive worship service, James exclaims, "That must have been quite a sight, seeing all those palm branches waving around. It must have helped the kids and adults experience what Christ saw when he rode into Jerusalem on that little donkey."

"Well, it did it for me!" Glendella says as she continues her reflection. "You remember that the Bible depiction of that scene says that Jesus praised the kids for being there. In fact, according to the telling in the gospel of Matthew, the grownups were jealous of the children. Glendella, pulls her cell phone from her pocket, and clicks on her Bible app, till she gets to this verse, which she reads aloud,

> *...but when the chief priests and the teachers*
> *of the law saw the wonderful things he did*
> *and the children shouting in the temple*
> *courts,*
>
> *"Hosanna to the Son of David," they were*
> *indignant.*
>
> *"Do you hear what these children are*
> *saying?" they asked him,*
>
> *"Yes," replied Jesus, "have you never read,*
>
> *"'From the lips of children and infants, you,*
> *Lord, have called forth your praise'"*
> (Matthew 21:15-16, NIV)

"Well, what happened after the service? Did the folks remember to pull their palms from under the seats or did the ushers have to collect and dump them?" inquires James, now in his voice as an usher who often has to help clear up the sanctuary after services.

"No, that's what is interesting to me," Glendella replies as she slips her phone into her purse. "Following the sermon, the pastor invited everyone to pull out the palm branches, notice the many fronds and then to use them during Holy Week to count their blessings."

"How're you supposed to use palm branches to count blessings?" James, now quite curious asks.

"He showed us how. He got one of the fronds from the vase on the front table and held up the palm branch. He told us to take a picture of us holding up the full palm branch after service that Sunday. Then he said we should wave the palm to remind us of Jesus. Then, he said, every day during Holy Week, to pull off three or four of those skinny leaves as we say out loud something for which we were thankful.

"By the end of the week, most of the branches would be bare."

"Yeah, and ..." James says to draw her out.

"But, he said, don't throw those stems away. Instead, stand that empty stem up in a pencil or pen holder in the kitchen or office where we could see the bare frond every day. That empty spine of the palm would remind us for the rest of the year of all our blessings and that with prayer and faith, we would have everything we need.

"After all, the Lord is equally our shepherd and the Lamb of God, and He promises to supply our needs! What we needed most was salvation and that is what we would be celebrating at the end of Holy Week – Resurrection Sunday, when Christ rose from the dead having died to pay for our sins."

"Wow!" James remarks, leaning back in his seat, then looking Glendella in the eyes, suggests as a question, "Think we should pass the idea along to Pastor Jackson? It's a pretty active way to count our blessings. He's into all that symbolic stuff to help model Bible teaching and behavior in ways that contemporary folks can understand. Um... let me check this out." He picks up his cell phone to see where one can get palm branches for a service like this. Then asks, "Isn't there someone at Beth-El who has a floral shop?"

"I don't think we have anyone who owns a store, but Maria Montpelier works at that flower shop down in the village. We got the bouquets for my sister's wedding through Maria's connections.

"You really think I should tell Pastor about this?"

"Sure, why not? This sounds like just the kind of modeling that will send home the message that we can be thankful for who God is and what Christ has done for us. And …And, you know, I think it'll be a great message to our kids and teens to know that Christ sees them and tells grownups to model their behavior of recognizing Christ and giving him praise.

"Hmm. Maybe I'll invite my mother and the teens to come here for that service. I usually try to get back to see her every few weeks. It's been a couple of years since they've been here. They stayed at a motel. I only got a one-bedroom apartment, you know.

"I think that'll be Spring break for them, too. "Yeah. I think that'll be Spring break for them, too. If they stay at my place, they'll be cramped, but they may like doing something different in a different town. You know I've only been here for three years and have not done all of the touristy things yet."

"Me neither. Maybe we can plan something that includes my niece and nephew. And, if the weather is nice, we can do a barbeque out in the back. I know Lillian and Louis wouldn't mind sharing their space for an occasion like this. And you know what?"

"What?" James can tell by Glendella leaning into the table that she has her planner hat on. He leans in, too, watching the excitement on her face to learn what she's going to say next.

"We still got one of those blow-up beds I brought with me when I moved here. Quentin and I used to pull it out when we had house guests. Lillian and Louis even slept on it once or twice. Claude stayed with the kids those weekends their parents came to see us at that time.

"Me and Quentin never had more than a two-bedroom apartment all the years we were in the service. That blow-up bed came in real handy for use in the second bedroom that usually served as an office for Quentin and a music practice room for me."

"Thanks, Glennie. That'll be real nice," James continues as he verbally visualizes lodging that weekend. "Hmmm. Mom can have privacy in my bedroom. My son can bring his roll-up camping mat. My daughter can use the blow-up bed. They'll think it's sorta cool for a couple of days. My front room is pretty spacious 'cause I don't have much furniture in there. I can sack out on the sofa. It's long enough.

"Celebrating Palm Sunday this way can work out for us all – you to be a hostess again, the church to celebrate in a fresh, authentic, and Biblical way, and me to have my family here for a few days. Thanks a lot!" James says with a little smirk, thinking of the plans he's going to have to make to accommodate extra people in his one-bedroom downtown apartment. Friends, like Glendella certainly can be a blessing. What kind of wife will she make? Do he want her to be more?

Shall We Worry or Hope?

Now that daylight savings time has been in effect for a month, Louis suggests that he and Lillian take their cell phones and do their marriage counseling journal work in the park. It's a week or so after Easter, and they are still flying high following the jubilant conclusion of the Lent celebration of Resurrection Sunday. As the couple sits in the car in the park across from Beth El Community Church, they gaze at evidence of rebirth in nature.

Louis recalls how much the two of them anticipated Spring for more than symbolic reasons. Then, he smiles remembering how astonished Pastor Jackson had been when Louis told him why he and Lillian had chosen that Fall holiday weekend to renew their vows and restart their marriage. That scene flits through his mind as he sits with his wife on one of the first really warm Spring days.

******

Pastor Jackson bows his head, murmuring, "Thank you, God! Thank you, God! I don't know how You did it, but You did!" He looks up and makes brief eye contact with Louis, then with Lillian, and asks,

"Well, when would you like to have this ceremony?"

"Thanksgiving Friday!" Louis and Lillian reply as a duet.

"Really? That's just a couple of weeks away. Why that holiday weekend?"

"Well, most folks have that day off from work," Lillian says with a giggle. "Not many of our members travel out of town till Christmas. And, most will be surfeited from Thanksgiving dinners, so we will have just a simple reception. We're not looking for presents, just their presence to celebrate our public commitment to be a Christian couple. Mother Grisham says the Hospitality Team will be delighted to help."

Pastor Jackson looks puzzled, unaware that the relationship between these two women had moved to this level.

Lillian notes his questioning eyes, and continues, "You know she's been counseling me in her role as a Titus 2 lady. We'd been studying that passage from I Corinthians 15 about my choices as a wife. She takes seriously Paul's teaching that older women should mentor young women in the church."

"Hmmm," the Pastor nods, again delighted that the congregants are being the church out of the church. And he comments with a smile, "Ah, she's taking the salt of the Word, out of the saltbox, as one could say."

"And …," more sedately Louis continues, getting back on plans for the ceremony, "Friday is traditionally payday."

"Payday???" Pastor asks, really puzzled now.

"Yes, according to the Bible," Louis explains, "Christ died for our sins on a Friday and paid ahead of time for the sins of the world. He knew we would commit some out of ignorance and others knowingly. So, Lillian and I would like to get married on this day to acknowledge that He paid for both our sins of adultery and unforgiveness."

Lillian continues, "We look forward to the resurrection of our marriage as we Christians celebrate Easter as the resurrection of our Savior. God, our Father, through the power of the Holy Spirit, is resurrecting our relationship in a more open way than either of us ever imagined last spring. What better way to celebrate Thanksgiving!"

Their pastor hops up from his chair, struts back and forth behind his desk, but by the third time, he strides around and approaches the two and gathers them into a hug. Lillian begins to hum, then sings the second verse of one of their favorite hymns, one that has taken on new meaning for each of them these past few months, "Standing on the Promises of God!"

Standing on the promises that cannot fail,
When the howling storms of doubt and fear assail,
By the living Word of God I shall prevail,
Standing on the promises of God.

'Louis!" Lillian draws Louis back to today. "Lookie! She points to a particularly active robin gathering twigs. Lillian reminds Louis of what the kids taught them when in elementary school their science teacher showed a video of robins building their cup nests.

"You know it's the female who builds the nest from dead leaves and moss and lines it with hair. I wonder where robins get that. Do they have arrangements with leftovers from barber shops and hair salons?" Lillian says, sipping from the thermos of tea they've brought with them.

"You're being silly, Lillian! But ... you know it's the male robin who feeds her during both the nest building and egg-laying. Just like me, right?" he teases, gently elbowing her in the side that is holding the thermos.

"Cool it, Lou! The cap is still off the top. You don't want me spilling this tea all over the seat."

He shakes his head, and she continues, "And, keep in mind, I've kept my job all these years. Thankfully, Virginia, as my CEO, chose to let me work from home so I could extend that second maternity leave when the twins were born. And what a blessing to have the childcare center on the first floor of our office building. Who knew that would be opened there? God certainly knows how to put us on the path to good things."

"You're right and you know, Babe, I was just kidding. Nature just continues to show us that God has a plan for family care, and it usually takes two. Now will you put down that thermos and pull out your phone? What has he sent us to talk about this week?"

"Say, Lou. Let's sit outside this evening. The sun's still out, but it's not hot yet. There's nobody over there in the gazebo. Let's go sit there. I'm sure we can get good signals on our phones. The teens are always over there, and you know they don't go nowhere they can't get them texts and posts."

"Sure, why not? Let's go. You gonna take that thermos with you? Got a cup in the holder over there? I could join your boozing! Those teas of your sister are making you a habitual drinker."

Lillian nods and grins as she reaches into the cache of cups she keeps in her car and hands him one with handles that pull out, and then pours him half a cup of her honey-sweetened tea. For coffee, they say, "No thanks. We eat our sugar." But, for tea, they usually add a teaspoon or more of that golden sweetener to the variety of herbal teas Glendella has introduced to them since she moved to town.

The spouses exit the car, Louis squeezes the key fob and waits till he hears the click before walking with Lillian along the cobblestone path from the parking lot to the wooden gazebo near the children's swings. There are no other folks here this evening since it's a school night and about the time most families are having dinner. He and Lillian had eaten a quickie meal of leftovers before coming to the park.

Once seated, Lillian pulls out her cell phone and taps the keys to the email that their marriage counselor has sent this week. All three of them are somewhat surprised at the bonds they built during just a few months of official sessions in his office.

After their final one last Fall, Dr. Manguel continues to send the bi-weekly prompts and Lillian and Louis find them just evocative enough to write or talk about the topics he sends. Lillian graciously confirms receipt and expresses their appreciation for his continued care even though he does not ask for or expect further payment.

"Well? What's he having us do this time?" Louis asks to get her going before sundown. It's still spring, and the sun will be setting in about an hour."

"Why don't you take out your own phone and look for yourself if you're in so much of a hurry?" Lillian chides as she looks up from her phone screen into the face of this man she's committed herself to for life.

Louis reaches for his phone, then looks at his wife as she chuckles because she knows he left it in the car. "No prob, Hon. I'll read from mine. Here's what the doc wrote,

"This week let's continue our experiment in exploring the future through three signals, one that worries us, one that indicates progress in some arena, and one that gives us hope. To focus your thinking this week, consider your three children. Who is worrying you, who seems to be making progress, and whose behavior gives you hope?"

"That's a toughie," Louis responds, now with his eyes closed as though he can see the answer behind his eyelids. "Hmmm. I could say something about each one using that prompt: worry, progress, and hope. You wanna start, Babe?"

"Well, I'm still worried about Louis because he hasn't been talking much about his plans for college this Fall. He's missed the early application date and is gonna have to depend on rolling acceptance dates. You know our state colleges fill up fast. But, I do see some progress in that he seems to be standing up more and skulking around the house less now. He's even been spending more time with Alysa. Did you know he offered to go shopping with her for her gown for the Senior Ball?"

"Okay, good start. Hmmm." Louis adds then goes on. "I'll do the same reflections for Alysa. I'm worried about her bouts of depression. Some days she's high as a kite, like the other night she told us about the paint colors she's using for the wooden necklaces she's making for the Spring GEMS' sales. Other days she looks low enough to walk under the dining room table without hitting her head!

"I'm not sure if it's because of us, her missing her sister, or her missing Claude. I do see progress, however, in that she has returned to participating in more voluntary GEMS events and seems to find joy in doing the grocery shopping for Mother Grisham. And, quiet as is kept, I feel some hope in what seems to be a budding relationship with Jabari. I've heard her on the phone with him when she's been working in the kitchen. They talk like friends. To me, that's a good thing."

"Well, yes. That's a sign of hope." Lillian confirms, "Lou Jr. does seem to trust him and that's a good thing, too. Guys know about the guys and if he thinks Jabari is safe for his sister, I'll follow his lead.

"Now, about Alvyra. Perhaps the only thing I worry about is that she'll find her time in France so gratifying that she'll want to stay longer. I miss my big girl and am eager to have her back home. On the other hand, I have seen significant progress, not just in her academics, but in her ability to talk with us about why she chose to leave in the first place."

"Lillian," Louis says sadly, "I had no idea that my coming out of the closet would send such recurring shock waves through our family, workplace, and church community! I really believed that because everyone already knew Claude and me, had seen our behavior at home, at work, and at church, that no one would have a problem with our being more open about the depth of our relationship.

"But seeing Alvyra squishing her eyebrows, shaking her head, and tearing up every time she looked at me nearly broke my heart. Learning that truth really struck her hard! And she couldn't hide or deal with it."

"Well, Louis, we're all different and thank the Lord, He provided a safe and reputable way out. She could have just run away. She's smart enough to make it in the streets!"

"Oh, Babe. Don't go there! I am so grateful that the opportunity to study abroad came up just at the right time. God certainly knows how to arrange our lives. Just gotta remain open to see and recognize which is his plan and which is ours. I never would have thought of a year abroad as an option for just one of our twin daughters. But, praise the Lord, it seems to be working."

"And," Lillian continues. "that's one of my reasons for hope. You know that she and Lawrence, Vincent's son who is a college sophomore, have been communicating regularly since our wedding ceremony last Fall."

"So, what's good about that?" Louis asks, somewhat alarmed at being upset. "We don't want her getting ideas about skipping college and hooking up with him! He's three or four years older than the twins! I can't imagine her not finishing high school here, not going on to college, but hooking up with that guy."

"No, don't be jumping to conclusions, Daddy Man! I'm glad that she is establishing a relationship with someone from a family we know. And, Honey, getting to know another male may help her understand the relationship you and I have. She will not be repulsed by the physicality as she has been in the past. Nor will she be tempted to try it out, too soon!"

"Oh Babe! You're scaring me. I forget about how tempting pre-marital sex is nowadays that teens know about birth control. What happened to my mom and what brought my birth to a teenage mother is less likely to occur. But, you know, I want my children, all of them, to save themselves for marriage."

Both parents sit quietly for a few moments. Each uses this time in the park to reflect on reasons they worry, noticing signs of progress and reasons for hope. They look up to the west and see that the sun is just starting to drop a few inches below the treetops with bright green leaves blowing gently in the evening breeze. Lillian agrees, summarizes, and exclaims about their discussion prompt this evening.

"Oh, Dr. Manguel. You always ask questions that get us thinking about our spousal relationships and our responsibilities as parents of teenagers." Then she looks up at the now setting sun, "Dear Lord, help us through here."

"You know He will, Lil. He always has. We have choices as we move forward having looked back on reasons to worry, ways we are pleased with progress and hopeful about the development of our children. It's all going to depend on ways they choose to put into practice what they're learning about living for the Lord!"

"Ok! Reverend Jackson Junior." Lillian teases and appeases. "I get it. We're to be attentive, model love, and teach them to do the same. So, what is our action step this week?"

He gathers her into a one-arm hug and pulls her up as he stands, "I think we better step lively and get back to the car. It's getting dark, and I'm getting hungry for dessert. Wanna stop at the coffee shop? That tea was okay, but a good cup of fresh-brewed decaf sounds just right for now!"

Can He Walk It Off?

Lou Jr. has had it! Alysa borrowed his car, the one Uncle Claude signed over to him when he left last year. Alysa has gone to do some grocery shopping for Mother Grisham. His teenage sister really seems to be taking seriously her commitment as a GEMS' girl to help out the senior citizens in their community. Today, Mom's car is in the shop, getting the tires rotated. Lots of his teammates have mentioned that they come "walk the mall" when the weather is inclement or unsafe for outdoor jogging. And, this crumby day, Louis has decided to do such a walk. So, he had to borrow Dad's car to drive through the slushy streets to the shopping center.

This brooding young man is on his third lap around the mall, so caught up in his own thoughts that he has not noticed the three times he has passed the men's clothing store where Jabari Mazari works part-time. Today he's been the greeter and has just returned to stand at the front door. By the time, Louis nears the store on his fourth lap, it is nearly time for Jabari's break, so he calls out.

"Hey, Man!" and watches several other men turn to see who may be calling them. Lou keeps walking, but since he's not walking fast, he's not out of earshot when Jabari calls again, "Hey, Fastball!"

Lou Jr., stops, wrinkles his forehead, knowing only fellow athletes from his high school call him that. Who at the mall would know that nickname?

He turns and sees Jabari, a senior in his class at the high school, beckoning for Lou to come across to his side of the mall. Lou had forgotten that his buddy worked at that store. Jabari glances around to see if his boss is watching, notices that he is, and so this teenage greeter stands up straight as though he is talking to a potential big- spending customer.

"Hello, Sir," he says and tilts his head toward the inside to alert Lou to go along. Lou, though surprised, gets the message, stands up straight, and looks closely at the trendy suits displayed in the storefront window.

"Um. Ah … Sir," Lou asks in character. "How about that shiny black sports coat there on the left side?"

"Oh, Sir. You do have good taste! That's one of our very popular styles this season. Please come in and try it on. I'm sure we have a size to fit your athletic physique," Jabari says a little louder than needed.

"Well. I don't have much time," Lou replies quietly. "I gotta get the car back to my dad who has got things to do this afternoon. But, yeah. I think I better come on in while I'm here." Lou falls into the role and follows Jabari over to the rack where different sizes of this jacket are hung. Jabari pulls two that look like they may fit and leads the way to the dressing room.

"Thanks, Dude," Jabari says as he hands the jackets to Lou who slips behind the curtains to actually try on these trendy sports coats. He's not really in the market, but it won't hurt to know what he's not buying today.

Jabari stands close enough to be heard as Lou shrugs off his wrinkly coat and slips on the jacket. "Hey, Man," Jabari says softly while still standing tall and straight. "I need to talk to you. Can I swing by after work for a chat?"

"What you wanna talk to me about?" Lou asks as he shrugs his shoulder to settle the too-big coat on his not-quite-broad enough shoulders. He slips off the large jacket, hands it out to Jabari, and pulls the smaller one off the hanger.

"I wanna talk to you about Alysa. She been acting distant lately. I already asked her to go to the Senior Ball with me, but I don't know, Man. Whatchu think? And you know what else? She made a scary statement about what struck her as their class was reading *The Sun Also Rises*. You know that book we read last year by Ernest Hemingway?"

"Yeah, I remember that book about those guys who used to be soldiers traveling down from Paris to Pamplimo or Pamploma or somewhere in Spain. What's she say, Jabari. Was it really that scary?"

"The city is Pamplona, with an "n", Louie, my man. It's that Basque town where they have the running of the bulls. That I know. About that quote. I don't know. But she said, "I can't stand to think of my life going so fast and I'm not really living it.""

"What you think she mean by that? She not considering suicide or nothing." This big brother's eyes glisten at the thought, " Oh God!"

"Nah! I don't think she's that desperate. Still, she has been acting odd. She used to be talking about her art all the time and about what she was doing better or different than Alvyra. I know Alvyra's over there in France, but Alysa still has her art. She got her friends and GEMS stuff, too. Ain't that enough?"

"I been noticing the same, Dude. She's been up and down at home, too, not sleeping much. I can hear her walking between her room and Alvyra's many a night. But she seldom actually goes in there. We gotta be careful through here.

"Mom and Dad are so busy focusing on themselves, I gotta watch out for my baby sister. Sure, come on over. I got a nice bedroom suite in the basement, but we won't have to go down there. We can have a leisurely lunch. I know we got some sliced lunchmeat in the fridge. But, my folks gotta go out to do something this afternoon. That's why I gotta get the car back soon. What time should I expect you?"

"That'll be great, Man. I get off at 1:00 today. I came in early to help stock the racks for the sale this weekend. Sure, I'll stop by the bake shop here in the mall and get a couple of those day-old donuts for dessert. You okay with that?"

"Sure, Jabari," Lou says, wiping his eyes with the corner of the jacket he'd flung on the chair there in the fitting room. "Hey, want me to come out and show you how I look?"

"Yeah. My boss is watching. He thinks I should be one of the salesclerks, so he'll be glad I look like I got a customer." Jabari asks a little louder, "Well, Sir. How's it fitting? Wanna step out and look at it in the full-length mirror?"

Lou Jr. puts on his Louis Senior smile, whips aside the curtain, steps out like he's a model for a private high-end fashion show, and strolls to the seven-foot-high mirror Jabari directs him to. Lou Jr. is stunned! He looks as good as he pretended to look.

"Well?" he stands, tall and straight, turning so he can see and be seen. "Looks good, doesn't it? How much you say this is?" He pulls up the price tag on the sleeve and nearly falls to the floor when he sees the price.

"Hold up, Lou, I mean, Sir! That's the full price." Jabari grabs the elbow of his friend and helps him regain his balance. "It's on sale this weekend. It'll only be half that till closing time tomorrow. This is a high-end fashion store. We don't have Sears and Roebuck prices here."

"Fifty percent or seventy-five percent off, this jacket is sharp but way, way out of my price range!" Lou explains, somewhat embarrassed that he hadn't taken where he is into consideration when he agreed to try on the sports coat. He tips up the other tag and notices the jacket is a Sioux Navy Sharkskin Suit Jacket and understands why $300 is considered half-price. It'll be years before he can afford to shop in a store like this, even during the deep-cut price sales.

"Well, now I know why the jacket feels so good and looks so neat. Even though I got on my casual sports shirt, I look like what my folks would call a "Dapper Dan", whoever the heck he was!" Lou is feeling lots better than he had when he arrived at the mall. Even though he's out of his range for shopping, he has a friend coming over for lunch and maybe they can come up with a plan to ease the emotional stress of his baby sister, Alysa.

She's been looking both distressed and depressed. Having spent so much time looking at the websites his coach had told him about when he, himself was feeling out of it, Lou Jr. recognizes some of the signs of a teen worried enough to do something dangerous or self-inflicting.

Yes, he knows she misses her twin, but they'd not been all that close this past year as each of them sought to find her unique place in the family and their school and church circles. Something is going on and he's the one big brother in this house. He's got to set aside "for me" and do what he can … "for her."

******

That next week, the weather is starting to warm up. The crabapple trees are budding, ready to blossom. Lou sees his neighbor, Ms. Andrea leaning against the white rail on her side porch, the one that curves around the left side of her house but gets little sun because of the tall junipers on the property border between her house and the Robertson. She's smoking a bogie, in hopes that the herbal medical cannabis will ease her arthritis a little more today. She probably wants to get out and work in her flower garden.

Andrea Mekonnen, holding the top rail on the porch banister, paces back and forth, inhaling deeply. She told the neighbors why she smokes pot, and some still are dubious. But they remain competitive. The neighbors on this circle set high standards for yard work. For some reason, they all do their own gardening, so often spend time chatting between chores.

She often takes time to talk with Lou Jr. who seems to be taking on more outdoor chores now that their play Uncle Claude has moved away. She had gotten used to seeing Louis and Claude trimming the plants, mowing, or raking the lawn. Now, it's Lou Jr. out there. He doesn't seem to enjoy the work, but he is careful about clearing up after he has mowed or raked.

It's a little warmer today, so Andrea beckons him to come join her on the porch for a cool boxed fruit drink. She'd heard him and brought out extra when she came out to greet him. Courteously, he waves to let her know he sees her, then calls, "Gimme a minute, Ms. Andrea. I gotta put this bucket of tools back in the garage. You know my dad. If things not where they supposed to be, the whole neighborhood is likely to hear him!" Lou chuckles.

Andrea has never heard such verbiage from her neighbor, but she smiles anyway. She waits for him to join her on the porch furniture her husband had pulled out when he was home last weekend. He's been traveling much more this year with the government job he got after their time in the Peace Corps.

"So, Lou. You have just a couple more months of school before you graduate. Where are you going to college?"

"I'm not going to college!" Lou responds emphatically, sounding like he's tired of telling inquirers that he has made his decision. He almost dares them to challenge but knows they will.

"Why not? I heard you're quite an athlete and you have pretty good grades, too. Can't you get a scholarship or something?"

"Yes, Ma'am. I got a scholarship offer, but I didn't accept it."

"What? Don't you know that half the seniors in the country would scorn you, especially if they're ones who've applied but did not get one?"

"That's their problem. Some high schooler's gonna be glad to get what I don't want right now."

"Right now. You think you can just tell people when you want a scholarship? That's not the way it works."

"I know, but college may not be for me. I gotta figure out what kind of career path I want to follow rather than waste time and money just to say I'm a college student. Well, may I have a box of that juice even if I'm not gonna be going to college. I'm kinda thirsty."

"Sure," she says handing him a box of juice and shaking her head. Another crinkle in the plans her childhood friend and now neighbor, Lillian will have to smooth out. Andrea hopes her younger teens won't put her through this now that they're about this age. She takes another pull on her cannabis, this time understanding why so many use pot for purposes other than medicinal.

"Lou, what do you think you want to do next year when you're no longer in high school?"

"Ms. Andrea. That's what I'm tryna figure out. Mom and Dad have not been asking, but I can feel their disappointment. I recall one time way back, that Uncle Claude had been reading a book called *The Purpose Driven Life*. That's the thing. I don't sense any specific purpose for me yet. Me and Lysa sometimes talk about life after high school, but I can't envision anything specific for me." He goes on, "I've even done some of those online career tests. But none of the results seem conclusive," he continues after pulling a deep swallow through the tiny straw he's inserted into the juice box.

This tiny container of Apple and Eve fruit punch is probably nutritious, but this juice is not quenching his thirst any more than considering his purpose is quenching his curiosity about next steps. What must he choose? What he wants or what his parents want? Will he recognize what God wants when he sees it? Will he be able to step out in faith, like Peter did...at first. He has to choose, then keep His eyes on Jesus.

Altar or Alter?

It's been nearly a year since the Reveal when Beth-El Community church members learned about the Robertson family. Pastor Sylvester Cedric Jackson and his parishioners have been challenged to put into practice what the Bible says about marriage and forgiveness. At first, the church members wondered why he had been preaching so much about love until he finally told them that it is only through the Agape love of Jesus Christ that they can continue as a unified body of believers who do not all see the application of Scripture the same way.

This Sunday, during their regular pastoral prayer, that time during the service when all who wish to give thanks for a victorious week or pray for repentance for not following the Word as they now understand it, the altar is full. From his place behind the podium, he cannot tell from their stances which are prayers of thanks, and which are prayers of confession. It really doesn't matter because God hears them all and honors the faithful prayers of those who come to Him with humble hearts.

Vincent in his role as Minister of Music has the gospel chorus singing what many still call a Negro Spiritual.

> Nobody knows the trouble I've seen,
> Nobody knows my sorrow;
> Nobody knows the trouble I've seen
> Glory hallelujah!

Pastor is continually amazed at how often the spirituals include "Glory hallelujah!" even when confessing difficult times. Now, he bows his head giving thanks for the fact that he has seen personal growth in himself and in many of the congregants who have continued to fellowship with them even as they have struggled to understand his teaching and preaching.

The choir sings softly as some of the prayer warriors or deacons and deaconesses as they are called in some churches, walk up to pray with those who have come forward. Most who've come to stand with those at the altar are older men and women who have been through times of temptation that they hear confessed at the altar. These listeners have learned to keep the confidence of those who open up and therefore have become trusted members of the congregation whose very presence helps petitioners "let go and let God."

The tension during services has diminished these past couple months. Pastor believes it's because members who do attend regular services, feel less judgmental scrutiny when they take the steps to come forward. They are coming to understand that they need not be ashamed to admit they need prayer.

Just last week, Pastor Sylvester had summed up his sermon in these words,

- "Be encouraged this morning. The Bible says in everything give thanks. Hold your head up. Pick your spirit up.

- "We spend too much time trying to forget our past, hide and cover up our past when our past is part of the pathway to our future.

- "God uses everything in our lives to make us better and to be our testimony to help others.

- "Our trash and tragedies become treasures and testimonies. Our messes, mishaps, and mistakes become our message and masterpieces in God's plan.

- "So, let's look up, get up and use what God has allowed in this trashcan of life to help others. By the grace of God, we are what we are, and we can't change it! Only God can.

- Give it to Him!

o   "Be encouraged!!! You're Ok!!!"

o   "God loves you just the way you are!!!"

******

Not long ago, one of the couples who had recently admitted they are dealing with marital issues, has come for counseling. That visit comes to his mind as he stands in the pulpit this Spring Sunday.

******

During that counseling session, Pastor Jackson slumps down into his large, black leather chair behind his equally large, mahogany desk, looking out the window at the just budding trees and sipping his herbal tea. He no longer resorts to rum as he had in his earlier days.

"Pastor," Horace, the husband says with bowed head. "I love my wife, but I don't like her very much right now. She knows why. In fact, we left our old church because so many people there started looking at us funny each time we arrived. Some even stopped sitting in the same pew with us. It was getting bad."

"Yes, Rev. Jackson," his wife, Penelope, continues, "It was hard for us to even believe it was a Bible-believing church 'cause the people shunned us even though we'd been going there for years. We were married in that church!"

Pastor Jackson is often torn between listening to the gushing of people he counsels and becoming a dumping ground of gossip. He is familiar with the Pastor of the church this couple has come from and he doesn't want to allow their experience with this fellow minister to color his relationship with this other pastor.

In fact, the two are in the local ministerial group that meets to address issues like this using the Bible as their guide. He is pleased to acknowledge that this pastor has not betrayed the confidence of this couple by talking about them at the ministers' meetings. He probably is sad that the couple has left for the reasons they now admit.

******

Refocusing his mind on the service in his own church, Pastor sings along with the next two verses.,

> Sometimes I'm up, sometimes I'm down,
> Oh, yes, Lord!
> Sometimes I'm almost to the groun',
> Oh, yes, Lord!

Pastor has raised his hands and because his own eyes are closed, he doesn't notice that many at the altar have also raised theirs.

> Altho' you see me going 'long so,
> Oh, yes, Lord!
> I have my troubles here below,
> Oh, yes, Lord!

Then, jerking a bit and opening his eyes, he remembers his role as Pastor and that the song is nearly through, knowing he's expected to lead the Pastoral Prayer. When he looks up, he notices that several at the altar and also in the audience are raising their hands on this final verse of admission and victory.

> What makes old Satan hate me so,
> Oh, yes, Lord!
> 'Cause he got me once and let me go,
> Oh, yes, Lord!

******

What a blessing to have a patient God who understands that Pastors are people. True, they serve as shepherds of a church flock, but these ministers also are men and women daily challenged to live what they preach and be consistent and considerate about what they teach.

During that counseling session with that couple, he'd been led to share something that Kamia, his wife had shown him just a couple of weeks ago. She also attends regular meetings of pastors' wives and had brought home a flyer about taking on new and challenging projects.

Since the Bible teaches that we are to love God and our neighbor as ourselves, it's important to develop a love for oneself.

The flyer Kamia had shared included this admonishment that he printed out and handed to Horace and Penelope.

******

Employing one of the strategies his professors at the seminary used when they want the students to think deeply about a topic while they are in the classroom, he offers this approach to this couple. He invites the pair to do a triple-reading. The first time read silently, the second time aloud, alternating readers, and the third time aloud, all three reading together, as one voice. He begins with an overview of his understanding of their marriage challenge and business plan.

"You two want to move on in your marriage and take over managing the commercial property that Penelope's parents have left to her. Horace, I can only imagine your surprise when you learned that your wife had gotten a little too involved with a high school classmate, who had been her father's manager these past three years. You feel betrayed. Unfortunately, that relationship had gotten a little too close and your marriage seemed to be in danger of dissolving. Now, praise the Lord, the two of you have committed to forgiving and moving on.

The couple sits a little stiffly in their seats, not sure where the Pastor is going next now that he has verbalized their problem and their goal.

"Horace and Penelope, please get a couple of pencils from the cup on the table over there next to the teapot. Yes, right there in the back corner. I think they're all sharpened. Kamia takes care of the office for me," Pastor says with a smile, acknowledging the help of his wife. Then instructs as he moves on in the session. "As you read, underline any words or phrases that puzzle or speak to you, or as our professor called it '*lectio divina.*'"

******

Once Horace had learned of the relationship between his wife and the former manager of the business, he hadn't even known his wife now owned, he suggested that man leave. The man resisted at first, but knowing who now held the reins of the business realized there was no business future for him there anymore.

Seeing the closed look on Penelope's face, that man realized there was no reason for him to pursue her anymore. He left. Yes, they did learn that he'd gotten a job with one of their competitors. With him gone, that temptation is out of the picture. But, the husband admits he still feels betrayed, and the wife admits she does miss her friend.

Now, in the consultation room with their new Pastor, Horace hands a pencil to his wife, who has handed him a book from the pastor's bookshelf. They center their papers on the closed books and read silently the single page of writing the pastor has given them. Pastor reads along silently, knowing that he's likely to see something he may not have noticed when he had read it earlier.

"Um... Pastor," he hears Penelope call out softly. He looks up, sees the couple eyeing him and realizes they've completed the first step.

"Oh, pardon me. I see something here for me," he admits, then the pastor invites, "Now, Horace, will you begin reading and stop at the end of the first paragraph? Penelope, you read the next lines, until the next paragraph. I'll read the next and we'll continue alternating readers until the end." This is what they read.

o   There are seasons and levels that require getting comfortable in your own skin before elevation comes.

o   Living at the intersection of joy and purpose is not just a matter of acumen and skill. Blooming at the intersection of joy and purpose requires radical self-love and acceptance. Why? Because what we do not love -- we HIDE and shrink away from.

o   Shrinking will always impair joy. Hiding will always constrict purpose.

o   Once I started loving ME, rooting for ME, and betting on ME like I did for everyone else -- everything changed.

o   What if the elevation and next level you seek is rooted in love? A deeper self-love. A healthy appreciation for your gifts and worldview. Radical self-acceptance rooted in love.

o   Love does not deny the need for continual growth or improvement.

o   Love is not a mask. Love is a release valve.

o   Love gives us permission to live boldly and to activate our dreams.

o   Love gives us the courage to influence and impact. Love ignites.

The three conclude their time together talking about words and phrases that puzzle and speak to them about their current situation. They encourage one another to let love empower their marriages and guide their next steps in terms of their business and his ministry.

Knowing this couple is depending on his counsel, Pastor Jackson closes with this confession and what he hopes is both insightful and inspirational.

"I may not be a blast from your past but allow me to whisper into your future. Humans are integrated beings. There is an inextricable link between the state of your soul and the work of your hands. To fully build what you dream, evolve in how you love the builder. That's you. The magic you wield in the earth is optimized when the work of your hands flows from a healthy and well-loved self – spirit, soul, and body."

******

Drawn back to the service as the choir is repeating a verse, Pastor detects that Horace and Penelope are among those with their hands up singing the fifth stanza that Vincent has the choir repeat,

> What makes old Satan hate me so,
> Oh, yes, Lord!
> 'Cause he got me once and let me go,
> Oh, yes, Lord.

Pastor Jackson leads the prayer, giving thanks and praise for the God who is teaching them all to love and let go. Then, Vincent, knowing the power of prayer and that most at the altar leave altered in positive ways, modulates the key and the rhythm having the choir sing and drummer beat to "Victory in Jesus!"

What Purpose or Plan?

A few days later, Lou Jr., in the basement storeroom, rambles through the box of books that Uncle Claude had left. Because he was not sure how much storage he'd have in his new digs, he had asked the family to allow him to store some of his belongings in the basement. He wouldn't need that many seasonal clothes in South Sudan, so if a situation arose, the family could use them or give them away.

Lillian, who wanted all signs of Claude to be gone, eventually consented to keep the winter clothing items and the books. It would be a waste to throw out reusable clothes and printed books. She admitted that, realistically, a time would come when these kinds of things could be passed along to those in need.

Now is one of those times. Lou Jr. needs some reading to help him clarify his thinking and articulate his thoughts. He thinks he is not cut out for college right now and he knows his parents are going to be disappointed when he tells them he already has turned down the scholarship offered by the state university athletic department. After his conversation with Ms. Andrea, Lou knows he has got to get his ducks lined up. He's going to have his own Reveal.

The young man recalls seeing in the box as he helped Uncle Claude pack, a book called *The Purpose Driven Life* by Rick Warren. When he had seen that book back then, Lou remembered Uncle Quentin telling him that Rick Warren's writing convinced him to stand firm on his commitment to the Air Force. At that time, when he was twelve years old, this preteen could not understand how a Christian who believed in the Ten Commandments which taught "Thou shalt not kill!" could be a soldier!

It was not until later that he learned how many of the Bible heroes and heroines were honored for killing. King David, especially, and Judith, a woman who had sliced off the head of an enemy and later Deborah, who helped start a war and later became the only female judge that Lou had ever heard about in Sunday school.

Uncle Quentin had clarified that it was not those Old Testament characters who served as his model. For him, it was Christ's teaching in the Sermon on the Mount, "Blessed are the peacemakers, for they will be called the sons of God," which influenced him. He committed his tech skills to helping his country avoid wars, not make them!

While he never would know, for sure, how successful he was, Uncle Quentin did serve for twenty-some years before his mysterious demise in Afghanistan. The family never learned the specifics, but Master Sergeant Quentin Gonzalez had been honorably buried in the Arlington Cemetery outside of Washington, D.C.

Though Uncle Claude and Uncle Quentin, both are men he admires for the same reason, making sacrifices to follow Christ, Louis does wonder about the specificity of those choices. Maybe flipping through that book and reading some of the sections will provide the rationales to articulate why these uncles found reading this book helpful in their Christian walk. Maybe, he, too, could find a way to unscramble his own feelings at this time.

"Oh! Here it is!" Lou exclaims as he stacks books on the nightstand next to his bed. On the book cover is a mature full-leafed tree with its roots showing and below them, what may be the subtitle, "What on Earth Am I Here For?" That is just the question Lou has been asking himself these past couple of months. He flips through the book and notices that this publication is a journal with questions and prompts to help readers like him answer that deep question that appears on the book cover.

As he scrolls on a website about the book, he notices this statement,

"God wants to redeem human beings from Satan and reconcile them to himself so we can fulfill the five purposes he created us for: to love him, to be a part of his family, to become like him, to serve him, and to tell others about him."

Wow! Lou thinks. This could be the mission statement for Beth-El Community Church! Though this young man does not recall Pastor Jackson quoting from this book, as one reflects on the kinds of sermons and ministry projects promoted at the church, most would fit into one or more of these categories. Hearing his neat-nik father in his mind, Lou Jr. restocks the box and returns it to the shelf in the storeroom. Of course, he has kept out the *Purpose Driven Life* book.

He calls upstairs, "Hey, Lysa! Come look what I found!" He knows she probably has not finished clearing up after supper and is still in the kitchen. So, he scuttles up the stairway into the kitchen and plops down on one of the stools at the breakfast bar and lays the book on one of the placemats mother leaves there to protect the countertop and the dishes, too.

"What you got there, Bro that got you all excited? I ain't seen you this up in a while," Alysa asks while bending to put the last of the dishes into the dishwasher now that she has rinsed the pots and pans. Yes, she knows that the dishwasher itself and the dishwasher soap disc they use are powerful enough to clean even the dirtiest of dishes and cookware, but their dad insists that they help out by rinsing everything first. So, they do.

When tempted to skip that step, they hear the sign on the wall speaking to them. It's one that Aunt Glendella and Uncle Quentin had sent as one of their housewarming gifts. This wooden plaque with a large golden sun in the upper corner is inscribed, "God is Watching! He loves you so much He can't keep His eyes off of you!" Anyway, clean dishes help support good health and that's a goal for them all.

"Oh, Sis. It probably ain't no big thing, but it is just what I need right now. You seen this before?" He holds up the book as she is hanging the dish towel on the hook inside the door to the cabinet below the kitchen sink. She jiggles the cloth a bit to make sure it will not fall off when she swings the door closed. Then she walks over to sit on the stool next to her brother pulled close enough to scan the book with him.

"What's it saying on that page?" she asks, seeing Lou is about ready to burst with excitement. Then she reads aloud, the subtitle, 'What on Earth Am I Here For?' What that got to do with us right now? You think you gonna find answers in a book?"

"Well. I really haven't read it yet, but what I see so far looks pretty good. It's a journaling book. Wanna do some of them with me? I gotta learn to put into words why I don't believe college is for me right now. It may have something to do with God's purpose for my life. I know we get to choose how we're gonna respond to His leading. But, you know, I'm not sure yet, what steps to take, but just know for now, it's not through the gates of academia."

"Listen to you!" his sister teases, bumping his shoulder with hers. "Well, which one of those prompts should we start with? This sounds interesting."

"I'm not sure. Why don't you pull out your phone and see if you can find an e-copy of the book? We can scroll on our own for ten minutes or so then see what hits us as we read. Wanna go sit in the living room? That's where mom and dad do their journaling. Maybe they left some inspiration in there for us."

"Nah. I don't wanna go in there right now. How 'bout we go into Vyra's room? She got a chair in there and I can sit on the bed. Yes, I'll straighten up the bedspread when we leave. You know, I really miss doing stuff in there with her. I've been avoiding going in there for multiple reasons!" she explains with a look in her eyes.

Her brother nods. He knows she's talking about their mom and dad still not sleeping together every night. "Sure. I'll meet you there in a minute. I'ma go back downstairs and get my tablet. I think I wanna write on that. Send me a text if you can't find a copy of the book online. I'll come back upstairs and we can read together. Okay?"

"Okay, Bro. Who woulda thought we'd be journaling at home like our parents? Are we gettin' that old already?" she says as she slides off the stool, pushes it under the counter and heads back to her room to get her own tablet. Why use a little ole cell phone when she can read and write more comfortably on the device she uses for schoolwork?

The brother and sister gather in their sibling's bedroom and talk about what they have read so far. They are tempted to call Alvyra to join them, then remember that it is nearly midnight in France and today being a school night, she probably is already asleep. They'll have to work as a pair for now.

******

Two weeks later, during Sunday supper, Lou Jr. asks, "Mom and Dad, can we talk after dinner today?"

"Sure, Son," Louis responds, curious that his son wants to wait. Though he wasn't a blurter, he usually raises any subjects during mealtime and the family discusses them right then and there.

"What you wanna talk about, Louie?" Alysa asks feeling left out again. "Can't we talk now or is this something private?"

"Alysa. Let's listen and not accuse," Lillian cautions, aware that the siblings seemed to have been getting along quite well recently. She doesn't want them to lose what they seem to have gained over the winter.

"Okay, okay!" Lou concedes. He takes a deep breath and unloads.

"I don't want to go to university next year!"

"What?" gasps Lillian, nearly knocking over her glass of water.

"What? Where's this coming from?" demands Louis.

"So, you're finally gonna tell them. Good for you!" Alysa exhales as though she is tired of carrying this secret about her brother, too.

"You're what?" Lillian asked with alarm in her voice. Has their family fallen completely apart?

"I'm not going to that state college in the Fall!"

"Why not?" Louis asked, with equal concern in his voice. "You got the scholarship, and you earned the grades. We've saved to fill in the gaps. What else is needed for you to attend your choice of colleges?"

"Well, my choice is to not go right now!" Lou Jr. exhales!

Knowing he needs a lead to keep going, Alysa inserts, "Why not, Louie? You're our big brother and we've been looking forward to bragging about you!"

"That's the reason, Lysa. Family first!"

"Ah, com'on, Son. What are you talking about?" Louis asks his namesake.

"Well, Mom and Dad, and baby sister, Lysa, next year will be the first time we'll all be living under the same roof again. I believe my purpose is to be big brother and buffer for my sisters."

"Big brother, I understand, but you don't have to put off going off to college to do that!" Lillian says, thinking she's relieved and released her duty-bound son.

"Yes, but to be a buffer, I should be home. Let me explain."

The family sits back, each eager to understand why Louis is backing off from the plan the family has had since his birth.

"I've been thinking about it a long time and have already declined the athletic scholarship the state college offered."

His parents gasp, but their son continues.

"As much as I like playing baseball, I don't want to have to play to go to college. I don't know what I want to major in, so I don't want to spend your hard-earned money studying who knows what."

Lou Jr. knew this news was going to disappoint his parents, but now he hopes, that they'll listen to his plan. So, he proceeds.

"I've been doing lots of research and have a proposal for you. Will you listen while I lay it out?"

"Sure, Son. You know we're in shock. You're our oldest and we've been planning and saving to support you all in four-year colleges since the days you were born. You've been doing well in school, what has changed?"

"I'm still doing fine in school, Dad, but that's because I like learning. I'm still curious and enjoy the intellectual challenges my high school courses offer me. But when people ask me what I'm going to study to become, I have no idea. So, here's my rationale, plan and proposal."

Lillian sees this is going to take some time, so she pours herself another cup of coffee. Her husband shakes his head when she holds the pot over his cup, indicating he doesn't want more. So, she sets the kettle down and leans back in her chair.

Lou sits up straight and begins, "I know that when a person gets to be eighteen years old, they should not expect their parents to support them financially. So, I have decided to attend community college and I've already been promised a job with Jabari's father. I can work full-time this summer and then twenty-hours a week once the new school year begins."

"You're not gonna be moving out, too, Louis?" asks Alysa as if she didn't already know. "Whew! You not gonna leave me here alone."

"Baby sister, you're never gonna be alone! Vyra's coming back and you got Mom and Dad. And…" he adds looking at his parents, "I hope Mom and Dad will agree for me to rent the lovely bedroom suite in the basement," Louis says with a smile and question in his voice.

"Rent! You don't have to pay to stay here!" Lillian exclaims.

"Mom, I'm over eighteen. I'm grown now and must start taking care of myself, but I can't quite afford it yet. That's my proposal. I know you and Dad have been saving for us to go to college. I'd like to ask you to loan me that money to go to community college. Then, let me pay 40% of my earnings for room and board, and I'll use 40% for transportation, clothing, and social life. The first 10%, of course is for tithes, and the remaining 10% is for savings. You always taught us to tithe and to save. Right?"

Louis now leans back in his chair, giving serious consideration to what his now grown-up son is suggesting they do to support him once he graduates from high school.

"And...Mom and Dad...in my research, I learned that most colleges and universities accept credit for general education courses taken at accredited junior colleges. Ours is, so that's what I have in mind. As long as I keep my grades up, I'd like to live here until I earn an associate degree. That's comparable to the first two years of study at a four-year college, isn't it?"

"Well, Son. It seems you have been thinking about this. This sounds like a thoughtful way to proceed, and your mom and I know that staying home and attending community college here in town will not be quite as expensive as living on campus at the state university. We just thought you'd be glad to be away and out on your own."

"Well, you're right there, Dad. I'd like to be on my own, but I can't afford it yet. And, as I've prayed about this and did my Bible studies, I believe my purpose is to stay and be Big Bro for another couple of years. So, I'd like your help for a couple more years, but I don't want to waste your money just so you can say you have a son in college. I know about bragging rights." Lou teases a bit.

"Hmmm," his dad continues. "You're right, too, that your mom and I would be proud to say that our son has done well enough to get a scholarship to attend a good college." Then, reaching across to clasp his wife's hand, Louis continues, "But, you know, I think we'd be just as proud to say that our son is taking giant steps towards adulthood by thinking of us in a financial way. He'll be continuing his education and he's teaching us, too, that he's learned the value of the hard-earned dollar!"

"And", Lillian inserts, "you know if you keep your grades up and maintain your athleticism, you may be able to walk onto the state college campus and get picked for one of the teams. They may even offer you financial assistance." Lillian is ever optimistic about others. If only she could be equally so for herself.

"So, Louie. What's this job with Jabari's father? You haven't said nothing about that to me," inquires Alysa after seeing that her mom doesn't seem to have any questions.

"Well, you know Jabari's dad bought the landscaping business where he's been working himself. It's mainly lawn care and Jabari's not the least bit interested in that right now. That's why he works at the men's clothing store in the mall. Well, during the summer, he and I will join his dad doing lawns and stuff, but in the fall, your boyfriend will be off to college. His dad wants me to work twenty or so hours a week, doing mainly record keeping and paperwork in the office."

Lillian, who has been working in an accounting office all her adult life, is leaning in, now, eager to learn what kind of office work her son will be doing, and ready to offer him tutoring should he need and ask for it. She asks,

"What kind of paperwork?"

"You know, keeping up with bills paying, planning promotions, and researching costs to stay current. His dad mainly does snow removal on contracts in the winter and doesn't need a full crew. So, Jabari will be heading off to college himself. He knows he wants to study legal stuff. Now that his dad's gonna have his own business, Jabari says he may major in business law."

"Wow!" Alysa exclaims, "My boyfriend's gonna be a lawyer! I wonder, is he keeping that a secret, too?"

"Hold on, Lysa. That's the thing. Jabari knows what he wants to study and can start taking general education courses that will funnel right into a major in pre-law and prepare him for law school right away. I have no idea what career path I wanna travel, so I don't wanna waste Mom and Dad's money … yet." Lou smiles as he says this.

"Well, Son, it seems like you've given this a lot of thought and the proposal you're setting forth makes sense," Louis says as he sits back and contemplates the next steps.

"And you know what, Mom and Dad? I settled on this proposal reading a book Uncle Claude left and a pamphlet Mom left in the kitchen last month."

"What do you mean? What book? What pamphlet?" Lillian bursts wondering what she may have left out that the kids should not be seeing.

Alysa jumps in. "Oh, Louie and I been reading and journaling using *The Purpose Driven Life* by Rick Warren. That book was in one of the boxes Uncle Claude left downstairs. It's a challenging read to say the least. The sub-title is "What on Earth Am I Here For?"

"And," Lou Jr. continues, "that flyer about the marriage retreat had that Jeremiah scripture about God having a plan for our lives. Well, the two of those readings clarified for me that I don't know the answer to either of those issues. Why I'm here and God's plan for my life.

"So, the fact that I don't want to have to play ball to keep my scholarship, and I don't know what I want to study makes me think of this plan of getting a job that will allow me to help with the costs of my living at home while I attend community college using some of the money you two have saved, seems like a good idea for now. Yes, I've prayed about it, and so I'm bringing it up to you. I respect you as my parents and if you say, I can't stay, I'll go."

You're Gonna Be What?

During this first Sunday in May for the regular semi-monthly family calls on Zoom to which Claude is invited to attend, Lillian comes prepared with questions to ask Claude. She's really curious to know how he's adjusting and praying that he is not conniving to try to get back his long-time lover, her husband, Louis. She finds that days go by and she feels confident in the attention she's getting from Louis, and other times she feels like he wants to be elsewhere, maybe with Claude. After all, the Claude and Louis of them have known each other longer than she has known either of them.

So, during the Zoom meeting that Sunday afternoon, the family is on as usual and Glendella has even brought down her tablet so she can join in this week.

"So, Claude, howzit goin?" Lillian asks. "How's the music at that church you're going to over there?"

"Lillian, would you believe, it is at church through the music that I'm learning the most? While English and Arabic are the two national languages, the majority of native Sudanese who attend our interdenominational church are Christians from the Dinka tribe who are employed in the international district of Juba; it's the capital city here in South Sudan."

Lou Jr., butts in and asks, "How you learning Dinka in an English-speaking Christian church?"

"Glad you asked, Louie," Alysa says. "That was gonna be my question."

"Well," Claude goes on. "It's really simple. The choir director has the song lyrics projected on a screen in the sanctuary, much like they do at Beth-El. But, when we sing hymns, he alternates the lyrics in English and in Dinka. So, we'll sing verse one in English, then verse one in Dinka. Verse Two in English, then in Dinka and so on."

"How does that help you learn the language?" Louis asks. He's the only member of the Robertson family who only took enough World Language courses to get into college. He has not studied any since. Even though racially and culturally diverse, the men and women on his team at work are English speakers, so he's been able to communicate effectively, and they get the jobs done equally well.

"Well, I see and hear the language every Sunday in three ways. In the songs, and in the preaching, and of course, in conversations overheard and shared after service. You see, the pastors alternate being the lead preacher. On first and third Sundays, the sermon is preached in English and translated into Dinka. On second and fourth Sundays, preached in Dinka and translated into English."

"Wow!" Alysa exclaims. "That church is really sensitive to its membership, honoring the languages, while teaching the Bible!" This teen is sounding more grown-up each week.

"And… you know what else?" Claude inserts and brings their attention back to him, startling them to the core when he announces,

"I'm going to be a Daddy!"

Whirling around the room are exclamations! "What?" "What?" "What?" and "Quoi?" comes through the Zoom screen from where Alvyra sits in her bedroom there in France.

"Claude! You promised," Louis nearly whines in disbelief.

With calm confidence, Claude replies, "So did God!"

"What you mean?" Lillian demands annoyingly. She's tensing up again, upset that she has forgiven, but still gets upset. When will it end?

"How a Christian gay man gonna be a father?" Lou Jr. questions and reminds, "In the video reveal at Beth-El, you said you took a vow of celibacy. You gonna go back on your word?"

"Well, haven't you ever heard of invitro fertilization?" Claude asks.

Of course, the teens whip out their phones to look up the term. Uncle Claude, who'd been a part of their education since pre-school, knows this behavior and gives them a minute or so to look it up. He watches the adults in the boxes on his screen, sitting in amazement. As they marvel, his mind reverts to the incident with that couple with whom he committed to sharing his sperm.

******

Claude is now living and working in Juba, the capital city of South Sudan. He has joined in fellowship with a congregation of Christians working in various government and educational groups committed to improving the life of the diaspora of Sudanese moving back to their home country. Many sons and daughters of what is known as the Sudanese Lost Boys got their education in the United States and Britain. A significant number of their offspring are keeping the faith of their fathers who encouraged their progeny to return to the native land of their ancestors.

Martha Nyandeng and Alfred Akech Majok are among those Sudanese descendants who met in Juba where they work near the US Embassy. She is a United States citizen and retains Obamacare even though she is living abroad. Alfred is from England; he too has health care. They work for one of the government programs located in the American Corner of Juba. Since their marriage, they both have drawn on the medical services covered by their insurance policies.

After Sunday service about five months ago, Claude had noticed the two of them walking back to their car, both with their heads bowed, not looking reverent, but sad. He was surprised somewhat because the sermon had been based on an exciting promise of God found in Ephesians.

Now to him who is able to do immeasurably
more than all we ask or imagine, according
to his power that is at work within us, to him
be glory in the church. (Ephesians 3:20-21,
NIV)

The service closed with an uplifting rendition of "Standing on the Promises." They'd sung all the verses jubilantly before the benediction and that fourth stanza had been so inspiring.

Standing on the promises I cannot fall,
List'ning ev'ry moment to the Spirit's call,
Resting in my Savior as my all in all,
Standing on the promises of God.
Nangtung dina jangji Allah.

Claude, walking to his car and humming the chorus, looks over to the next row of parked vehicles and sees Martha standing leaning on their little car. She's weeping, her colorful scarf-wrapped head resting on the bronze metal roof and her husband's arm around her, his hand patting her shoulders. Following the nudge of the Spirit, Claude calls, "Can I help?"

Alfred turns, gives him the eye, and says, "This is not your business! Stay out of it. Go on home."

Claude, hearing the words but feeling a tug from Alfred, keeps walking. He puts his arm around Alfred, who stiffens and shakes off that arm. "No!"

Claude snaps his finger, recalling that the congregation knows he is a gay man. Oh no! He wonders if Alfred thinks Claude is "coming on to him!" In the church parking lot! Puh leeze! Then, feeling a strong nudge of the Spirit, Claude steps back, then invites. "Come on. Something's the matter. God has an answer. Let's walk a bit and talk. You can trust me. You know me."

By this time, Martha has straightened up and takes her husband's hand. She wipes her tears with his sleeve, and he chuckles. That sound seems to drive away the worry, and the couple agrees to walk with Claude.

As they stroll along the deserted weekend downtown street, they surprisingly dump what they've been keeping secret for so long. Claude learns that they are sad because another month has gone by, and she has not conceived. Just yesterday, they got the results of a test that Alfred is infertile. He, too, is feeling down because he cannot contribute what is needed to fulfill one of his wife's fondest dreams, to be a mother.

Claude blurts, "No problem. She can have sperm of mine!"

The couple stops in their tracks, "What! No way José!" Alfred exclaims. "We're not that desperate! I will not have my wife sleeping with nobody else. Especially not a White man! Our women don't have to do that anymore!" Martha leans into her husband's shoulder shaking her head in disbelief.

"No, no … no!" Claude clarifies right away. "You know I'm gay. I'm not into women. Anyway, we can go scientific, the medical route. You both are college graduates. You know about surrogacy and in-vitro fertilization. Right?"

The two pause a moment, and then nod their heads. "Yeah, but we're Black. What are we gonna say if the baby turns out light or white?" Martha asks. But Claude senses she may go along if her husband consents. But will he?

"That's all I need!" exclaims Alfred, whirling away, but not releasing his wife. "Blokes and other folks laughing at me behind my back, saying I couldn't satisfy my wife, so she started sleeping with a man from our church. How is that going to look?"

"No problem," Claude replies in a calm, soothing voice. "Just tell the truth. You love your wife so much that you want to give her her heart's desire. So, you give her the gift of sperm that you got from a brother in the church."

"Man!" Alfred sighs. "You make it sound so easy." He shakes his head in disbelief.

"What about the baby, when kids at school start teasing our child about not looking like he's ours." Martha keeps asking questions about the future, knowing what could possibly happen in a heterogenous community where they are likely to reside.

"No problem. Tell the truth. The child is a gift from the Lord." Claude exclaims, then asks wistfully, "And, please, let me be the uncle. After all, you are my sister and brother. Right?"

By this time the trio is in front of one of the few cafés open on Sunday so, Claude in his inimitable way, invites them in for lunch. The three of them go in and share a meal, and by the time they are sipping coffee with their dessert, the Majoks obviously are giving serious consideration to this peculiar answer to their prayers.

They'd been "Standing on the Promises" for years. They've heard sermons during which their pastors have pointed out that God sometimes says "Yes." and then gives exceedingly abundantly beyond what they could ask or imagine. Then, the sermon this morning seemed to be untrue for them … until now.

Claude has been thinking the same, until now. Lord, you know how much I miss the Robertsons. You've given me an opportunity to stay connected virtually while staying away physically. Now, I may get to be both an uncle and a daddy of sorts right in my new hometown. You are something else! Thank you, Lord.

After a couple of months, the couple, having given Claude's offer serious thought, make an appointment to meet with their pastor to let him know how they sense God answering their prayers. The pastor asks many of the same questions about dealing with the gossip that is sure to arise. Then, the couple reminds him of what he preached about the gift of love.

This couple is willing to have their child this way. Their decision to accept his gift of sperm for use in a medical way seems to be giving Claude such joy. He can keep his commitment to his lover and to his Lord to remain celibate!

The pastor shakes his head and then nods it. It is gratifying to see how his parishioners are literally applying the Word. The three pray, and before the couple makes their way back to their car, Alfred has his cell phone out, calling Claude.

The three visit the doctor who performs the tests, arranges the collection of eggs from Martha and sperm from Claude. When the second test tube shows the egg is fertilized, invitro fertilization works, the implant takes place, and now Martha is pregnant.

******

"Uncle Claude!" Alvyra's voice on the Zoom screen draws him back.

"What!" he exclaims a little startled to see his American family in little blocks across his laptop screen. Then remembers where he is and what he has just told them."

"When's the baby due?" asks Alysa, picking up on her twin's thought, though Alvyra is online from France.

"We're having a Valentine's month baby!"

"Whoopee!" the twins cheer, but Lillian and Louis both are a little more solemn than jubilant. This is good news, right? The three are getting what they want, right? The two young people will have one new baby, right?

Lou, Junior, verbalizes what they all may be thinking, "Well, they could have twins. They do run in the family. Right?" No one says a thing.

For about half a minute, Claude watches them looking at each other, then they burst out laughing. He even notices the Frenchy chortle that Alvyra has picked up since studying abroad. Even Lillian manages a little smile.

Signing off the meeting, Claude says, "What a blessing to be Nangtung dina jangji Allah.

The family nods, "Yes!" They've picked up the fact that Claude is speaking Dinka here saying, "Standing on the promises of God!"

Is This an Imitation of Life?

Tears drip from Alysa's eyes. As a self-selected novel for her Junior Year Honors' English class, she chose to read *Imitation of Life (1933)* by Fannie Hurst. Their assignment is to read a novel published during the decade their great-great-grandparents had been teenagers. As an interdisciplinary assignment, they are to create a multi-media presentation about the ways the SEPs of that historical period are experienced by characters in their chosen novels.

Their teachers expect these students to cite real evidence about the social, economic, and political milieu of the time their novel is set or was published. Depending on where in the world their ancestors lived during those formative years, the students can draw from what they learned in their sophomore World History classes or in their current United States History classes. In the Hurst novel, Alysa is reading, Peola, the main character, is a woman of African descent, who is successfully employed. Peola's skin tone allows her to pass for White.

Alysa has finished reading the book and tonight she is watching the movie version of this novel. It's a second film based on the book, and in this one, the main character is called Sarah Jane. Still, it's a wrenching story that pulls at Alysa's heartstrings. In the scene now, a darker-skinned person knocks at Sarah Jane's door. When she opens it, startled at who is standing there, she looks both ways, sees no one in the hall, then hurries this older woman into the room, and quietly shuts the door. It is her mother! They have not been together in years!

The story continues showing the young woman torn between acknowledging and denying to herself that this is someone she knows and loves. She weighs what she will have to give up if she admits to the world that though she does not look like one, she is a woman of African descent who would be shunned if this fact were known.

Alyssa wonders if this has been her father's quandary. Had he been afraid he and his family would be stigmatized if the community, church and people in their workplace had known of his bisexuality? That's who he is. Why must one deny or hide the truth? Her daddy is honorable, faithful to God, wife, and family.

Should she, his teenage daughter, despise her father for who he is as Sarah Jane seems to loathe her mother? The daughter stands in front of her mirror exclaiming in her mother's presence, "I am white! I am white! I am white." She isn't really. Alysa's dad has told them the truth! Should Alysa question his integrity? She has had no reason to do so in the past. Why now?

Just last evening, while doing homework in her bedroom, she had taken a break to get a snack. Alysa had stopped in the hallway when she heard her parents talking in the front room.

******

Alysa peeks around the corner but doesn't move.

Lillian turns her laptop screen so Louis can see it more clearly, and states reflectively, "This documentary about that exhibit at the London Tate Modern Museum is really something else!"

"What do you mean?" Louis queries as he flips up his phone to see if any work calls have come in. There have been none. Good. He turns to his wife to admit, "I caught a few glimpses and only noticed lots of splashes and swashes of different colors, textures, and mediums."

"You're right! Modern art looks like that to many people with an untrained eye," she teases. "But what about the sculptural installation by that Portuguese artist, Leonor Antunes?"

"You mean the one you showed me with all those strings and knots?"

"Yeah. That one. Wait a moment ... Let me scroll back to that section of the video." Lillian pulls the laptop closer, swiping her finger across the touch keypad. Back, back, back, then pauses the screen showing the exhibit that had struck her as metaphorical of her life.

"This one!" she squeals. While she turns the device to angle the screen so he can see what she means, Louis slides out of his seat and kneels next to her so they can view the screen together.

Both look, each hoping their spouse sees the artistic depiction as something positive about their life and future together.

Rather than continuing to the kitchen for her snack, Alysa tips back to her bedroom. There she has left her computer tablet open to the online screen where she'd been viewing a video of *Imitation of Life*. Alysa quickly searches for the artwork of Leonor Antunes displayed in that exhibition at the Tate Museum.

On the screen she sees, suspended from the ceiling in the gallery, a square five- or six-feet metal frame from which hang woven strips, ropes of different diameters, textures, and colors, and something that looks translucent, almost transparent. Wow!

Alysa, the artist, muses a bit, admiring the creativity of this woman, then tiptoes back down the hallway to the front room, where her parents are sitting. She stops. Her mom is talking.

"... And that narrow red curtain in the back, see it there on the left."

"Yes. It must have taken a lot of patience to weave that lengthy panel of what looks like knitting yarn. How do you see that skinny thing representing us, Sweetie?" curious Louis asks encouragingly. He's so glad Lillian has begun to verbalize her thoughts more readily. Now that the truth is out, he's eager to discover and to explain whatever may be puzzling her about his choices to keep so much from her.

She continues, "To me, that could represent how our nice family life shielded you and Claude from public censure for over seventeen years."

Louis exhales and smiles, "I'm glad you describe those years of our life as nice. Go on. Wait! There are two red fabric panels. See the one back there on the right? Hmmm. Those two panels could be the parallel lanes of bisexuality."

"Um… hmmm. Yes, you could interpret them that way. And in front of those two panels are those two jumbled knotted ropes hanging side by side. That's where we are now. Still the same dusky red colors as the thread in the panels in the back. I'd say that on some days the red stands for anger and fiery resentment, mine for you and you for Claude. The large knots and soft open spaces also could stand for the love of God demonstrated in different ways."

"Okay. I can see where you're going with this," Louis intersperses, reflecting. "Love led Claude away in a Christ-modeling act of sacrifice. That could be one set of those ropy thingies. And the other could be of us tied together, empowered by a Holy Spirit and Agape love. What about that filigree curtain of gold threads hanging in front? What's that saying to you?" he asks to keep her talking.

But Lilian says nothing. She leans back in her lounge chair, tightening her knees to stabilize the laptop.

That is when Alysa bursts out, startling them both. "Mom! Daddy!" Alysa, grinning broadly, joins her parents. She drops to her knees next to her dad and leans in to point to the screen. Though she'd only glimpsed the exhibit on the computer tablet in her room, she'd also been drawn to the open weaving of golden squares hanging as the front of the artwork, nearest the viewers standing in the museum.

"That golden piece is us! Our family. Doesn't the Bible say, God will restore us, if we trust Him? Doesn't gold represent a bright future? Something valuable to treasure? Even though those strands in that structure are not as tightly woven as in the red curtain in the back or as tangled as the separate knotty ropes in the middle, the golden strands are still connected."

Alysa now feels her dad's arm around her waist and her mom's hand on her shoulder.

"See, Mommy! See, there, Daddy! The translucent golden panel is the one piece that extends from left to right in front of them all. We can't hide our past, but we don't have to stay there, either!"

Now, Louis rises from kneeling on the floor, returns to his lounge chair, and leans back, exhaling, "Listen to our prophetess!"

Alysa gets up and squishes onto the chair with her mom, with just one hip on the cushy front corner. Having been acknowledged as a prophetess, Alysa continues as an historian.

"Mom, will you do a quickie search for images of kintsugi art?"

Open to the way the conversation is going, Lillian turns the computer toward Alysa. "Here. You know how to spell that word. It sounds like it may be Japanese. You do the search."

As Alysa taps in the word using the flat keyboard, Lillian looks at Louis, raises her shoulders, and tilts her head. Louis responds with a nod agreeing they can just let things flow.

"Here. Look at this!" Alysa invites, swiveling the computer so both parents can see. On the screen is a bright green ceramic vase that looks like it had broken and then been glued back together with swirls of gold showing along the cracks.

Louis opens the way for the explanation, "... and?"

Lillian conscious of the time and that tomorrow is a school day, says in her mommy mode, "Quickly, Lysa. What's the connection between that antique Japanese ceramic vase, 20th century Portuguese string art, and a 21st Century African American family!"

Chuckling, their daughter responds, "I'll let you two figure that out since you're telling me to go to bed without actually giving me the order." Alysa, the teacher, now daughter, hops up, turns and asks, "Can I get a quickie snack first? Studying and teaching have made me hungry!" With that, she skips into the kitchen, grabs a cookie and a glass of milk, and sits on a stool at the ceramic-top breakfast bar. She can hear her parents, sensing they know she still is listening.

"That Alysa!" proud daddy Louis remarks, then summarizes, "But, you know, she may be right about the triple link among the Old Testament and the artwork we've seen today. Just as kintsugi art, made of broken ceramics soldered together with melted gold, is valued, so our choice to remain a united family may become valuable to our children."

******

Now, this evening after, Alysa, recalling her dad's summary, nods her head, praying that this will indeed prove to be true for the Robertson family. But, they'll have to wait for her twin to return before the restoration begins. They'll have to pull disconnecting Lou Jr. back in, too. Now, however, she senses the gold of love is warming them all and will be at the right temperature to do its part in just the right time.

When that happens, she won't be tearing up for the same reasons as Peola in the Hurst's novel, *Imitation of Life.* In the movie scene's close, Sarah Jane does weep, saying goodbye after choosing to live physically apart from her beloved mom. Ah, Alysa thinks. This young lady, denying her heritage will still be connected by love in much the same way as Alysa had sensed last evening viewing the golden weaving by the artist, Leonor Antunes, and heard in the conversation between her parents. Love is the golden thread of life.

Does Poetry Speak for Me?

One misty afternoon in May, Alysa stomps into the kitchen, holds out a damp plastic grocery bag and calls out,

"Mom, look what Mother Grisham sent you!"

Lillian sets down her feather duster and walks into the kitchen wondering what could be in a package from Mother Grisham, the wise old lady from their church who promised to keep her in prayer. Alyssa has been doing grocery shopping for the lady since she fell on an icy patch in the church parking lot following their Christmas service. She's not been as agile as she'd been before and graciously accepts the help of the teenagers in the GEMS group.

Ms. Delphi, their group's leader encourages the young women in this Bible-based, non-denominational social group to help whoever, whenever, and wherever opportunities arise. She calls them GEMS, diamonds in the rough, sharpening their skills as they put into practice what they learn in their weekly afterschool meetings at the church Delphi attends.

By the time Lillian gets to the kitchen, Alysa has slipped off her wet sandals and left them on the pad near the back door. She's tiptoed across the cool tile kitchen floor and laid the bag on the breakfast bar. Lillian notes it was one of those thin white bags many stores now provide for customers to carry out their groceries. She first fingers the bag, then opens it, and pulls out a slender turquoise book called *Marriage Connections: Faith Based Stories and Poems.*

"Ah! This is a book Mother Grisham told me about," she explains to Alysa. "One of her friends, Dr. Annette M. West collected these stories from women across the country and published it last year. I wonder what Mother Grisham thinks is in it for me." Lillian flips through the book and notes photos and biographical sketches of the contributors, then sets the book back on the counter. "I'll look at it later."

Then she gives her attention to her daughter who still stands there watching her mother's response to this gift.

"How is Mother Grisham today? She still making you use coupons?"

"Yeah, Mom. She hands me an envelope with a ten and three twenty-dollar bills, her grocery list and four or five coupons. The list is marked with stars for the things with coupons. There's a check next to items I can substitute if her first choice is not there. So, I have no excuse for getting anything wrong. She does the math, so I always have enough money."

"Does she check the groceries when you bring them into the house for her?

"Not anymore. She did at first. And she used to count the change. And you know what? She used to check the expiration date on the cans and boxes. She says she doesn't want food to spoil in the closet before she gets around to using it. But, she trusts me now, and just gives me a hug when I've taken in the last bag.

"Sometimes she offers me a cup of hot chocolate, too. I said no, today. But, Mom, I really could use something special to drink. I got a ton of homework to do this afternoon," she says, looking at her mother more intently as though she's anxious, but really wants to admit what she's feeling. "You know those AP exams are next week. It's tough studying alone. I'll be glad when Alvyra's back. We didn't always get along, but we studied real good together."

"Sure, Baby. I'll fix you one of those smoothies. It'll be refreshing and healthy. What kind do you want today? I got some carrots, bananas, and apples. You want a tea, milk or yogurt base?"

"I don't care. Whatever you fix will have to hold me over till dinner! But, Mom, don't overdo it with the oats!" Alysa teases as she eases out of the kitchen.

"Okay, you go change out of those damp clothes. I'll finish dusting in the front room, then come fix you a smoothie."

Alysa, starts to walk away, then turns back to ask, "Mom, does Mother Grisham know that you and Dad are planning to go on that marriage retreat this summer? That you decided to go ahead and pay the higher summer fee 'cause you want to be here for Lou, Junior's end of the school year events. Well, I guess, since you're not gonna have to spend so much for his college tuition this Fall, you may as well spend it on yourself," she chuckles, knuckles her mother gently on the shoulders and walks through the kitchen and down the short hall to her bedroom.

On the way, she glances to the right, sees the sunlight shining through the raindrops on the window of her twin's bedroom. Oh, she sighs, I'll be glad when Vyra's home. We could peep into the living room where Mom'll be reading that book.

That evening the twins would have seen Lillian doing just that.

******

After dinner, Louis had gone downstairs to talk privately with his son. He says Lou still wonders if he will become more attracted to males than he is now to females. He has a girl friend who will attend the Senior Prom with him, but they don't spend much time together, what with studies, sports, and her job as a waitress. Lou has said he wants to remain celibate until he marries, but he really isn't finding that all that hard to do. The guys at school talk a lot about their triumphs and he finds he doesn't care.

Lillian stretches out in her lounge chair up in the living room to pass the hour or so before their regular evening devotions time. It is that forty-five to fifty minutes the couple still devotes to reading their Bibles and journaling. Sometimes they talk about what they read, often they just let the Spirit speak to them individually, then they move on.

Over the past few months, they have conceded that they are at different places in their Christian walk, and that sometimes the Scriptures speak to each of them in different ways. They have decided not to argue or try to convince the other he or she was right or wrong, just to remain open to being taught. God knows their hearts and what they need. Sometimes it is quiet support, not challenge.

As Lillian flips through the book, she stops at the section on poetry. One title, "The Man with the Holes in His Socks" catches her eye. It's a couple pages long, but just a few words per line. Hmmm. Could be interesting. She tilts her head towards the twins' bedrooms and hears Alysa talking to someone on her cell phone. She hasn't heard her husband come back upstairs, so believing she has privacy, Lillian does what her teachers taught her to do with poetry. Read it aloud. She reads,

"The Man with the Holes in His Socks"

Sitting across from him on the sun porch
      Noticing those holes
      in the bottom of his socks,

Listening to the birds
      Chirping their evening reports
      to their parents,

Hearing the squawk of the ducks
      Teaching their ducklings
      to swim upstream,

I wonder what it would be like.

What would it be like
      to have no one to talk to,
      no one to report to,
      no one to tease about the holes
      in the bottom of his socks;

      no one to interrupt my reading with,
      "Hon. You've gotta listen to this." or
      "Just a minute.
      Have you heard this one?"

      Listening to the roiling of the stream
         just outside the sunroom window,
      Hearing the water tumble
         down the man-made rock croppings,
      Pausing as the mourning doves coo
         across the way,

I wonder what it would be like.

What would it be like to be able
        to finish a chapter
        without being interrupted,
        without learning something new
        about something
        I never knew was important,
        something I'd never
        even thought about before,

without realizing
        how fortunate I am
        to hear from the man
        with the holes
        in the bottom of his socks, say

"Babe. This won't take long?" or
"Betcha never hear this anymore."

Sitting across from him,
I watch the sunbeams
        Streaming through the blinds,
        Slipping over his shoulder and
        Warming my toes,
        Signaling that day is ending,
        I wonder what it would be like.

Then, I smile to myself,
        not having to wonder,
        glad I don't have to wonder,
        thrilled I don't have to wonder

What life would be like
        without the man with the holes
        in the bottom of his socks.

Lillian laughs a bit thinking, this could have been written about me and Louis. He doesn't sit across from me like the narrator describes in the poem, but he does sometimes walk around with holes in his socks. He does interrupt me when I'm reading, too. That's poem is fine, but what about these other stories. There must be something in here that Mother Grisham thinks I should be reading.

She continues to skim, stops at a couple of the stories, and reads them through. By the time Louis joins her, she realizes that Christian marriages are distinctively different. What each of these stories seemed to be saying is that if one stays centered in Christ, one can make it through.

When her husband joins her, she does read aloud the poem to him. Louis laughs and recognizes himself in many of the lines. But he particularly appreciates the closing stanza that his wife reads as though it is her wish, too.

> Then, I smile to myself,
>   not having to wonder,
>   glad I don't have to wonder,
>   thrilled I don't have to wonder
>
> What life would be like
> without the man with the holes
> in the bottom of his socks.

Time for Spring Fling?

It's Mother's Day and Vincent has the Beth-El Community Church congregation singing "Faith of Our Mothers." It's both a traditional song and a reminder to those who have grown up in families of faith, but equally to inspire current moms to be this kind of mother. During the fellowship snack time following morning worship and before the grade level Sunday School classes for kids and teens and topic choice classes for the adults, Pastor asked each person to share with three different people three valuable lessons they learned from their mother.

As expected, some of those in the group get weepy, not just because their moms have transitioned to their afterlife, but also because some parishioners do not have a good relationship or a good memory of their own mothers. Anticipating this emotion, Pastor had encouraged them to consider mother figures as well. These may be aunts, neighbors, even classroom teachers or professors.

It is this third category of mother figures that surprises so many as they recall the less familiar third and fourth stanzas of that opening hymn.

> Faith of our mothers, guiding faith,
> For youthful longing, youthful doubt,
> How blurred our vision, blind our way,
> Thy providential care without.
>
> Faith of our mothers, guiding faith,
> We will be true to thee till death.

Few in this group have gone to Christian schools and are amazed at how many of their public and charter schoolteachers exhibited the characteristics described in that third verse. Several of the Beth-El members had been among those with youthful longing and youthful doubt, with blurred vision blinding their way and many in this group of parishioners had gotten into serious trouble. But, today, praise be to God, some of the folks sharing stories today find themselves giving thanks as they acknowledge the guidance they received from their various schoolteachers.

Equally powerful about this time of fellowship is that teachers in the group are being reaffirmed about the role they have in the lives of their students. Their influence with their students goes beyond that of simply passing along course content information.

The fourth verse reverberates with long-time Christians who have been torn about their religious and cultural traditions and the trajectory of their contemporary church.

> Faith of our mothers, Christian faith,
> In truth beyond our stumbling creeds,
> Still serve the home and save the Church,
> And breathe thy spirit through our deeds;
>
> Faith of our mothers, Christian faith,
> We will be true to thee till death.

As they snack on the goodies provided by the church hospitality team, sip the coffee or tea they have chosen as a hot drink, or suck on straws of cooled boxed juices, teens and adults recall that just a little over a year ago their congregation had learned the Robertson family story. It was just a couple of Sundays after Mother's Day. They had wondered what the guys' parents' would have thought had they been in the service that Sunday of Memorial Day weekend. Had they already known about Claude and Louis?

That Sunday, last year, the Beth-El church family had experienced the video of Claude admitting he is gay and that he is following the example of Christ to give up for those he loves so that they all can go on living for Christ the way they now understand the application of the Word.

Neither he nor Louis deny their sexual orientations, but both have committed to celibacy in terms of intimate relationships with anyone outside their marriage. That led to that marriage commitment in a second church ceremony once Lillian and Louis decided to remain married. Just a couple of months ago, Beth-El members had learned in a surprise announcement that Claude will become a father through surrogacy and invitro fertilization. This church family has been wowed by the ways God is fulfilling His promise of blessing them above and beyond what they could ask or imagine.

Of course, all the wrinkles are not yet out of the tapestry of life. Some of the long-term members continue to grapple with what they had been taught and what they now are seeing differently, but still seems to be accurate application of the Word. They find themselves loving anyway. Before now, the term agape love had meant little. Now they are learning they are to love and let God be the judge of the hearts of others.

From what they see, the Robertsons are demonstrating Biblical behavior in the ways they are behaving towards each other and responding to congregation members. So, though shocked to learn of the behind- the-scenes relationship of Claude and Louis, who believed deep down in their hearts that they are as God made them, the church members are finding they can love anyway.

The Beth-El group would be delighted to learn what else has happened since that Mother's Day month a year ago.

So very evident of the change in the past year is the fact that Mother Ruby Robertson is welcoming the greetings of her son, his wife and their children. Few folks in her home church had known her backstory because her parents had helped to hide it. What had they hidden?

******

Ruby Lynn, the teenage daughter, a PK, had been considered royalty among her peers. The teens in the neighborhood seldom invited this preacher's kid to typical teen gatherings. The boys knew not to even think of touching her or asking her out. Her parents, however, had consented to board, Jamal, an African immigrant college student to aid his adjustment to living in the United States. Ruby was lonely and warmly welcomed Jamal to the family, to her heart, and all too soon to her bed. Her parents, initially furious at the young people, insisted that they get married right away, just in case she was pregnant. She was.

The congregation members could count, and the pastor did not want to deal with the gossip he knew would ensue. This teenage mom had raised her child in her parents' home because Jamal died just a few months after the birth of their son, Louis Jamal.

It was later, during his freshman year in college, that this young mother learned of her son's sexual orientation. She was appalled! Within months, sold the house, married an older man, and moved to California. She feared the fallout about her son's queerness more than the public scorn her parents had shielded her from when he was nearly born out of wedlock.

She had despised Lillian for nearly two decades because she thought Lillian had known that her husband is gay. And further, from what the grandchildren had revealed about their mother, Mother Ruby could not imagine how a woman of Lillian's character could have consented to marry a gay man.

Lillian hadn't known about either: his sexuality or his relationship with Claude. But, when she did learn, she forgave him, consented to remain his wife, and, to start fresh, even had a second marriage ceremony.

It was during a phone call, inviting her to that event last Thanksgiving weekend. that Mother Ruby had learned the facts to which she had been closed for so long. Over the years, Lillian had simply thought it was money and business that had kept her mother-in-law from visiting her only son. Between the Reveal and the phone call, Lillian decided that Mother Ruby had kept herself apart because she had known and disapproved of the relationship between Claude and Louis. Both mother and wife had been in the dark!

Now that she opened herself to learning the truth, Mother Ruby has forgiven herself for blocking their love. She understands Spring Fling in a new light. She knows the Urban Slang dictionary defines "spring fling" as: "A casual relationship between two persons who are usually attracted to one another. This can involve puppy love, sex, or perhaps just "hooking up".

It was just this past Fall that Mother Ruby Roberson had finally released the judgmental attitude about her son's sexuality. She has found that that letting go of hate, lets in light. She has flung away the negative feelings and is hooking up with her family. Like many at Beth-El Community Church, this grandmother now finds that celebrating Mother's Day can be a joy.

Summer Choices

Finally, Time to Blossom?

For the first time in nearly a year, the Robertson family is seated together in the sanctuary. And, since this is not the Sunday that the gospel choir sings, Glendella is seated with them, right next to the twins Alysa and Alvyra, with Lou Junior, like his dad, is seated in the end seat. Alvyra has returned a week early from her year abroad in France to attend the graduation ceremony where Lou Jr. received an honorary mention as a scholar-athlete.

Not many of the seniors on the sports teams earn a spot on the honor roll. Still, the principal had been reluctant to include this young man in that portion of the graduation ceremony once he learned Louis neither accepted the athletic scholarship nor planned to attend a four-year institution of higher learning. Ms. McBride, the long-time English teacher who had recently retired, happened to be subbing the day this list of honorees had been posted in the faculty room.

When she hadn't seen Lou Jr.'s name, she confronted the principal and convinced him to acknowledge what the young man had accomplished rather than deny him for what he was not planning to do … yet. She, too, had heard the comments in the faculty lunchroom. Theirs is one of those high schools that brags about the number of graduates who get accepted to quality accredited colleges. Louis Robertson, Jr. not being among the college bound in this graduating class has caused some to question who is at fault.

Recently, the Beth-El congregation has noticed many things about this family. Lillian and Louis have resumed sitting side-by-side. For months, the troubled couple had been sitting on opposite ends of the fifth row of seats on the left side of the sanctuary, where the family had sat for years, but for months, with Alysa and Louis seated between them.

Observers also have noticed that Lou Jr. does not often seek out female companionship during fellowship time after service, nor does he regularly bring one to their Beth-El social events. He comes stag. So, it's not surprising that the dubious members are questioning his sexuality.

Both Louises do, too. But neither is worried. The father and son have privately talked about the questions that keep popping up. They both are trusting what they are learning as they read and reflect on Scripture will provide them with the guidance they need. After most of those conversations, the father and son pray together, asking for the Lord's leading and seldom let the thoughts become worries. They do, however, continue to wonder. What next?

Today, Alvyra is wiggly. Her body is not yet back on the Eastern time zone, but she is delighted to be back home. She can hardly wait to go out with Lawrence, Vincent's son, who has been communicating with her since Fall, when her parents renewed their wedding vows right in this church. He, too, is home from college and is now up in the sound booth, resuming one of the roles he had filled for years when he was a high school student. He'd texted her last night and asked her to go out with him for dessert. He knows the Robertsons have their special Sunday meals and that few reasons convince the parents to excuse one from attending.

Alysa, the other twin, is coming to terms with the fact that her Sunday School classmates keep looking at her oddly since she shared those slides about Jesus' being tempted by Satan. When she had explained how she "saw" those images, the teens had squinched back as though she is contagious. Thankfully, Jabari seems to understand the power of imagination and has not seemed put-off by her creative side. He's coming to dinner today and she is really looking forward to that, even though he'll probably be a little late because the church he attends is on the other side of town.

Today, Glendella is dressed in a little more casual attire than she usually wears on Communion Sunday. She, too, has a date. James Milton, who is ushering today, has asked her to be ready to leave right after service for a short drive across state.

This friend, a widower whose son and daughter live with his mother has invited Glendella to ride with him to pick up his teenagers to come spend a few days in town with him. Now that their high school and college exams are over, neither has to return to class; their grades are posted online, and none of the Miltons have required end-of-school year events to attend.

Though she won't forget her husband of twenty-five years, Glendella, the recovering widow is now eager to move on with life. And, these past months, her relationship with James seems to be blossoming, but both remain cautious. Because today's round-trip journey is short enough to make in a single day, she has consented to accompany him. And, if Jim Jr. his long- legged son sits sideways in the back with his sister, Regina, James' Nissan Versa will be spacious enough for the four of them to ride comfortably.

So, no reason to spend the night and no worries about uncomfortable situations that could tempt Glendella and James to break their vows to the Lord to remain celibate as long as they remain single.

Lillian, seated this Sunday next to her husband, pulls out her phone to log on to the Bible app when Pastor announces the Scripture for the day. She smiles when a photo pops up of Alysa and Jabari, taken before they left for the Spring prom. Both are smiling from ear to ear. But the main reason Lillian keeps this photo on her phone opening page is that Alysa's eyes are smiling, too. When Lillian tilts the phone so Louis can see, he, too, smiles, probably for the same reason.

For so many weeks, the family has watched the emotional swings of the youngest member of their household. However, a f t e r having that fit on the bedroom floor, then a few days later, being inspired by viewing the modern artwork of Leonor Antunes, things seemed to be turning around. Her parents are seeing signs of revival, the return of her sunny self.

Alysa has continued with her volunteer work with Mother Grisham and making attractive wooden jewelry, but the activities no longer seem to be fillers, but fulfillers. Now that her twin has returned home, the family is praying that the two of them will reconnect in positive ways and have a triumphant senior year of high school, each supporting the other as each continues to do her own thing.

Today seems like a positive sign. Alvyra and Lawrence have extended a welcome for Alysa and Jabari to join them, and the younger twin is stoked. She has come to appreciate Jabari who has been so supportive of her brother during this tumultuous final semester at school. Thankfully, the baseball team coach did let Louis play this spring even though Louis had turned down the scholarship offer to the coach's alma mater.

The disappointed coach had written a glowing recommendation for Louis. But, he also wanted to continue having a winning record, so he permitted Louis to play this term. The surprised teammates followed their coach's lead and welcomed "Fastball" to his final season at the high school. Alysa and Jabari attended many of the home games to cheer the team on to the finals. Though the other team had won, Fastball had made them work hard for that win.

******

This June morning, following the regular order of first Sunday services, the choir sings a classical hymn. At first, members of the congregation look puzzled. Why have Pastor Jackson and Brother Vincent, their minister of music chosen this particular song for a Sunday the church family usually celebrates communion, taking the bread and wine in remembrance of Christ's sacrifice on Calvary.

> Guide me, O Thou great Jehovah
> Pilgrim through this barren land;
> I am weak, but Thou art mighty,
> Hold me with Thy pow'rful hand.
> Bread of heaven, Bread of heaven,
> Feed me till I want no more;
> Feed me till I want no more.

However, as the worshippers pay attention to the words of the second verse as it is projected on the screen in the front of the sanctuary, these lyrics take on fresh meaning.

> Open now the crystal fountain,
> Whence the healing stream doth flow;
> Let the fire and cloudy pillar
> Lead me all my journey through.
> Strong Deliv'rer, strong Deliv'rer,
> Be Thou still my Strength and Shield;
> Be Thou still my Strength and Shield.

The song over, the singers are taking their seats, wriggling a bit as they reach for their cell phones on which most store their Bible app and follow along during service. Then, once they're settled, the Pastor stands and strides to the podium, nods a warm greeting to his wife, Kamia, then with another nod, signals the tech team in the booth over the rear doors of the sanctuary. Soon, the congregation sees projected, up on that same screen, this familiar Old Testament scripture:

Trust in the Lord, with all thine heart, and
lean not on thine own understandings, In all
thy ways acknowledge Him and He will
direct thy path. (Proverbs 3:5-6, KJV)

This Bible passage on Communion Sunday? Why? Then, as Pastor Jackson expounds in a humble confessional homily, the choice of that earlier song and this sermon text become clearer. Listeners begin to nod as though the pastor's comments are speaking for them, too. They lean in when, as usual, Pastor Jackson moves along from an Old Testament to a New Testament scripture. This week, he has chosen.

I thank my God every time I remember you.
being confident of this, that he who began a
good work in you will carry it on to completion
until the day of Christ Jesus. (Philippians 1:6,
NIV)

As the sermon unfolds, Pastor acknowledges his questioning about the direction of his teaching and counseling. He mentions no names, but because so much has been public in the lives of several of their brothers and sisters, many in attendance today are aware of some of the incidents to which their pastor alludes. After all, they are family. And family talks.

When he closes the sermon, Pastor nods again to Vincent who begins playing one of the regular songs sung during communion, "Nothing but the Blood of Jesus!" The attending deacons and deaconesses come forward to accept and hold trays with the blessed elements of bread and wine. Following the directions of James Milton and the other ushers, the congregation marches from the rear to the front to pick up their little cups of wine and snippets of matzo, the kosher crackers being used for communion this month. The communicants step lively to this invigorating song,

What can wash away my sin?
Nothing but the blood of Jesus.
What can make me whole again?
Nothing but the blood of Jesus.

Thankfully, the words are projected so all can see and sing along as they march forward, and again once they return to their seats. They sing all four verses before jubilantly singing the refrain.

For my pardon this I see:
Nothing but the blood of Jesus.
For my cleansing this my plea:
Nothing but the blood of Jesus.

Most have been served by the third verse. They remain standing, ready for the ordinance, holding the upraised matzo to eat and the cup ready to drink.

Nothing can for sin atone:
Nothing but the blood of Jesus.
Naught of good that I have done:
Nothing but the blood of Jesus.

By the fourth verse, the whole congregation stands at attention, singing the closing verse and the refrain, then following the lead of their pastor, they will take the elements, one at a time,

This is all my hope and peace:
Nothing but the blood of Jesus.
This is all my righteousness:
Nothing but the blood of Jesus.

Refrain:

O precious is the flow
That makes me white as snow;
No other fount I know;
Nothing but the blood of Jesus.

The celebrants now eat, chew, swallow. Sip and swallow and then look back up to the front, gazing at their church shepherd. He stands ready to close the service with a brief benediction. Before doing so, though, he repeats the interrogatory sentence that closed his sermon: "What would Jesus do?" during which time Pastor Jackson had outlined the decision-making process.

Now, he quotes verse four of the lyrics from "I Have Decided to Follow Jesus!" delivers the benediction and nods once more to Brother Vincent, who leads the choir singing this song of commitment as the congregation recesses to the fellowship hall.

The world behind me, the cross before me;
The world behind me, the cross before me,
The world behind me, the cross before me;
No turning back, no turning back.

******

Because Glendella and James are leaving right away to drive across the state to pick up his children, they do not stay for snacks. Instead, they head right for his car, but the fragrance of the blossoming flowers in the park across the street cause them both to stop in their tracks.

It almost feels like they are experiencing synesthesia, a rhetorical device or figure of speech where one physical sense is described in terms of another. It's like this couple is in a movie with special effects where one can "see" a fragrance infusing a space. The aromatic lilacs in the center of the park stand majestically, their blossoms hanging on just a little longer than usually are seen in June.

The men's group at the church on the other side of the park has taken on the task of keeping the flower gardens weeded and watered and their work is blossoming beautifully. The beds of red, pink, white, and yellow peonies and carmine and wine-red day lilies seem to shout, "Look at me!" The purple salvia sways in the wind and the hearty daisies tilt from left to right, looking confident that just their being there draws attention to the beauty of God's creation.

Once in the car, snacking on the cookies and sipping the iced tea Glendella had packed, James asks. "So, what's on your agenda for the kids this week? I heard Louis say he and Lillian are going to be out of town. You overseeing the kids?"

"You better quit that, James! You know they'd be upset hearing you calling them kids! Well, since Lillian and Louis have decided to go on that marriage retreat, Virginia, her work-buddy told them about, I've decided to have another combo-family cookout in the backyard. Your mom and the teens seemed to enjoy that when they came during Spring break.

"It's time for your son and daughter and my nieces and nephew to get to know each other better. My three have been asking if they're going to be relatives, soon. Will we two become one …one big family?" Glendella blushes wondering if she's jumping the gun, suggesting something she wants, but a leap this man may not be ready to take.

"Is that a hint that you're open to the idea of marrying me and mothering my children?" James blushes but confesses. "Since she is nearly finished with high school, it's not likely Regina will want to leave their grandmother. But, Jim, Jr. may come to work for us at the university. As my son, he'll qualify for an employee family discount, so he can continue his college education here."

Glendella, disappointed, shrinks back, leaning against the side window. She had thought they were further along than this. Oh well.

James goes on. "Well, Glennie, I have been thinking about marriage and blending families, but am not really ready to get into the specifics. This is a toughie for me. Let's just enjoy the trip. We'll see how things go this weekend when we're all together."

Feeling a sense of the maybe, Glendella sits back up straight, leaning a little to the left, nearer to James, who keeps his eyes on the road ahead, and continues talking.

"Oh-kaaaay!" he says as though giving in, but glad to do it. "Yes, I do believe it is time for us to see if God wants us to marry. We've got lots to consider. It's not just you and me. What will it take to become a brand-new blended family?"

Glendella relaxing a bit, wonders too. James doesn't really need a wife after all this time. He's gotten used to being single. His kids are nearly grown; they don't need a new mother. Does he believe he can marry for love again? Does James even love me, or am I just a convenience?

******

Back at Beth-El, inside, during the fellowship time following the service, folks are verbalizing their lack of surprise that Pastor's key verse was from Proverbs 3:5-6. It has struck a chord with so many in the congregation. Conversation is confirming that when they ask for guidance, they are feeling more confidence in their purpose and God's plan.

Through the teaching and preaching this past year or so, more members are coming to understand better the concept of choice and consequences in terms of their relationship with God, their Creator. Since the birth, death, and resurrection of Jesus Christ, they can just choose to follow His model, to leave judgment to God and to follow Paul's teaching in multiple epistles, to just love.

But, most importantly, as Pastor reminded them when sharing his thoughts on Philippians 1:6, it is God on whom they can depend. He keeps His promises. Father God has sent the Holy Spirit to be with them all, through today and on to the end.

This morning, just over a year since that alarming Reveal about the sexual orientation of Louis and the sacrificial departure of Claude, the listeners still sense the presence of this Spiritual Companion. He flowed during the service and remains among them as they sip and chat. The church family has been observant. More and more, like the Robertsons, these Beth-El brothers and sisters are choosing to trust agape love, in kintsugi style, to heal and weld them together as a blended, united church family.

Time for Reflection

Reflecting on the Writing and the Message

1. What is the significance of the title? The sub-titles? Do you find them meaningful? Why or why not?

2. How would the events in this story have played out differently in a different historical time or place?

3. What motivates the actions and reactions of different characters in this book?

4. Which characters remind you of someone you know, have observed, or have read about in other fictional works?

5. How do the way the characters see themselves differ from the way others see them?

6. Did your opinion of the characters change as you continued reading the story? Why?

7. Were there times you disagreed with a character's actions? What would you have done differently?

8. Which moment in the story evoked your strongest emotional reaction? Why?

9. What ideas does the author illustrate? What message is the author sending?

10. How would you summarize this book using the Five W's and H? Who? What? When? Where? Why? and How?

Reflecting on Historical and Theological Ideas

11. What historical incidents did the author present that intrigue or inspire you to explore more?

12. Which seemed strongest to you: the novel's nuanced characters, the spiritual world, or the compelling plot?

13. What helpful fresh revelations or new thoughts did you receive as you read? In what ways does your knowledge of the topic expand?

14. In what ways did reading the lyrics of hymns enhance your understanding of characters, plot, and message?

15. What part or parts of this book did you find encouraging? List some adjectives that describe your overall impression. What is your main takeaway?

About the Author

Anna J. Small Roseboro is a wife, mother, veteran educator, and author of books in multiple genres: fiction, poetry, and textbooks for teachers.

She currently uses these experiences and skills as a mentor and writing coach. But, because she is first and foremost a child of God, she intentionally shares her Christian journey in devotionals, anthologies, and online interviews. This story about the Robertson family reflects her passion for storytelling and belief in the power of collaboration. Anna Roseboro invited more than a dozen contributors who consented to share fictional narratives in the persona of characters in the prequel, *TWO, ONE, NOW THREE: How Can It Be?* (2022), in the follow-up novel, *THREE, TWO, ONE: Time to Run?* (2023) and she has alluded to or included those characters in this current work of Christian fiction, *CHOICES. CHOICES? CHOSEN!*

Anna is the author of this intricate novel because others have shared secret eyes of life, based on their experiences, observations, and reflections on sexuality, family life, and Christianity.

Anna J. Small Roseboro also is the author of other publications that may be of interest to readers of this novel.

ON ZION'S HILL: Funny and Frank, Fanciful and Faithful (2015)
SWEETHEARTS OF ZION'S HILL: A Collection of Stories, Editor (2016)
EXPERIENCE POEMS & PICTURES: Poems that Paint/Pictures that Speak (2018)
RAINBOW REMINDERS: What the Colors Tell Us (w/Nancy White) (2022)
RAINBOW REMINDERS: Cross-Curricular Activities (2022)
CINDY AND SANDY: Learn about Elephants (2022)

See more on her website https://ajsmallroseboro.wordpress.com.

www.ingramcontent.com/pod-product-compliance
Lightning Source LLC
Chambersburg PA
CBHW080842120626
46553CB00009B/2533

* 9 7 9 8 9 9 1 1 5 9 5 0 0 *